AN

ANGLO-SAXON PRIMER

WITH

GRAMMAR, NOTES, AND GLOSSARY

Owing to the antiquity and rarity of this book, certain pages are regrettably absent, and readability is compromised due to the blurring of the original text. If you possess any insights regarding the availability of these missing sections, kindly inform us. Your assistance is crucial in ensuring the completion of this significant work for the benefit of future generations.

AN

ANGLO-SAXON PRIMER

WITH

GRAMMAR, NOTES, AND GLOSSARY

HENRY SWEET

GYAN

Published by

GYAN

Gyan Publishing House
5, Ansari Road
Daryaganj, New Delhi-110002
Phone: 011-47034999, 9811692060
E-mail: books@gyanbooks.com

Distribution Network
gyanbooks.com
India, USA, Canada, UK, Australia

ISBN: 978-93-7014-744-7 (PB)

First Published, 1900

2nd Impression 2025

Printed at: Gyan Press, Delhi.

AN ANGLO-SAXON PRIMER WITH GRAMMAR, NOTES, AND GLOSSARY

Author: HENRY SWEET

AN ANGLO-SAXON PRIMER

SWEET

Clarendon Press Series

AN

ANGLO-SAXON PRIMER

WITH

GRAMMAR, NOTES, AND GLOSSARY

BY

HENRY SWEET, M.A., PH.D.

Sixth Edition

Oxford

AT THE CLARENDON PRESS

1890

PREFACE.

THE want of an introduction to the study of Old-English has long been felt. Vernon's *Anglo-Saxon Guide* was an admirable book for its time, but has long been completely antiquated. I was therefore obliged to make my *Anglo-Saxon Reader* a somewhat unsatisfactory compromise between an elementary primer and a manual for advanced students, but I always looked forward to producing a strictly elementary book like the present one, which would enable me to give the larger one a more scientific character, and would at the same time serve as an introduction to it. Meanwhile, however, Professor Earle has brought out his *Book for the beginner in Anglo-Saxon.* But this work is quite unsuited to serve as an introduction to my Reader, and will be found to differ so totally in plan and execution from the present one as to preclude all idea of rivalry on my part. We work on lines which instead of clashing can only diverge more and more.

My main principle has been to make the book the easiest possible introduction to the study of Old-English.

Poetry has been excluded, and a selection made from the easiest prose pieces I could find. Old-English original prose is unfortunately limited in extent, and the most suitable pieces (such as the voyages of Ohthere and Wulfstan) are already given in the Reader; these I could not give over again. But I hope the short extracts from the Chronicle and the Martyrdom of King Edmund will be found not wanting in interest. For the rest of the selections I have had to fall back on scriptural extracts, which have the great advantages of simplicity and familiarity of subject. The Gospel extracts have been transferred here from the Reader, where they will be omitted in the next edition. The sentences which head the selections have been gathered mainly from the Gospels, Ælfric's Homilies, and the Chronicle. They are all of the simplest possible character, only those having been taken which would bear isolation from their context. They are intended to serve both as an introduction and as a supplement to the longer pieces. They are grouped roughly into paragraphs, according to the grammatical forms they illustrate. Thus the first paragraph consists mainly of examples of the nominative singular of nouns and adjectives, the second of accusative singulars, and so on.

The spelling has been made rigorously uniform throughout on an early West-Saxon basis. Injurious as normalizing is to the advanced student, it is an absolute necessity for the beginner, who wants to have the definite results of scholarship laid before him, not the confused and fluctuating spellings which he cannot yet interpret intelligently. Even for purely scientific purposes we require a standard of comparison and classification, as in the arrangement of words in a dictionary, where we have to decide, for instance, whether to put the original of *hear* under *é*, *íe*, *í* or *ý*. The spelling I here adopt is, in fact, the one I should recommend for dictionary purposes. From early West-Saxon it is an easy step both to late W.S. and to the Mercian forms from which Modern English is derived. I am glad to find that Professor Sievers in his admirable *Angelsächsische Grammatik* has also adopted *ie* instead of the later *y* in *hierde*, *hieran*, &c. That I give Ælfric in a spelling slightly earlier than his date is no more unreasonable than it is for a classical scholar to print Ausonius (who doubtless spoke Latin with an almost Italian pronunciation) in the same spelling as Virgil.

It is impossible to go into details, but in doubtful or optional cases I have preferred those forms which seemed most instructive to the student. Thus I have preferred keeping up the distinction between the indic. *bundon* and the subj. *bunden*, although the latter is often levelled under the former even in early MS. In the accentuation I have for the present retained the conventional quantities, which are really 'prehistoric' quantities, as I have shown elsewhere (Phil. Soc. Proc. 1880, 1881). It is no use trying to disguise the fact that Old English philology (owing mainly to its neglect in its native land) is still in an unsettled state.

In the grammar I have cut down the phonology to the narrowest limits, giving only what is necessary to enable the beginner to trace the connection of forms within the language itself. Derivation and syntax have been treated with the same fulness as the inflections. In my opinion, to give inflections without explaining their use is as absurd as it would be to teach the names of the different parts of a machine without explaining their use, and derivation is as much a fundamental element of a language as inflection. The grammar has been based throughout on the texts, from which all words and sentences given as examples have, as far as possible, been taken. This I consider absolutely essential in an elementary book. What is the use of a grammar which gives a lot of forms and rules which the learner has no occasion to apply practically in his reading? Simply to cut down an ordinary grammar and prefix it to a selection of elementary texts, without any attempt to adapt them to one another, is a most unjustifiable proceeding.

In the glossary cognate and root words are given only when they occur in the texts, or else are easily recognizable by the ordinary English reader.

All reference to cognate languages has been avoided. Of course, if the beginner knows German, the labour of learning Old English will be lightened for him by one half, but he does not require to have the analogies pointed out to him. The same applies to the relation between Old and Modern English. To trace the history of the sounds would be quite out of place in this book, and postulates a knowledge of the intermediate stages which the beginner cannot have.

The notes consist chiefly of references to the grammar, and are intended mainly for those who study without a teacher. As a general rule, no such references are given where the passage itself is quoted in the grammar.

On the whole I do not think the book could be made much easier without defeating its object. Thus, instead of simply referring the student from *stęnt* to *standan*, and thence to the grammar, I might have saved him all this trouble by putting '*stęnt*, 3 sg. pres. of *standan*, stand,' but the result would be in many cases that he would not look at the grammar at all—surely a most undesirable result.

Although I have given everything that I believe to be *necessary*, every teacher may, of course, at his own discretion add such further illustrations, linguistic, historical, antiquarian, or otherwise, as he thinks likely to instruct or interest his pupils.

My thanks are due to Professor Skeat, not only for constant advice and encouragement in planning and carrying out this work, but also for help in correcting the proofs.

In conclusion I may be allowed to express a hope that this little book may prove useful not only to young beginners, but also to some of our Professors of and Examiners in the English language, most of whom are now beginning to see the importance of a sound elementary knowledge of 'Anglo-Saxon'—a knowledge which I believe this book to be capable of imparting, if studied diligently, and not hurriedly cast aside for a more ambitious one.

HENRY SWEET.

CONTENTS.

GRAMMAR.

The oldest stage of English before the Norman Conquest is called 'Old English,' which name will be used throughout in this book, although the name 'Anglo-Saxon' is still often used.

There were several dialects of Old English. This book deals only with the *West-Saxon* dialect in its earlier form.

SOUNDS.

VOWELS.

The vowel-letters in Old English had nearly the same values as in Latin. Long vowels were marked by (ʹ), short vowels being left unmarked. The following are the elementary vowels and diphthongs, with examples, and key-words from English, French (F.), and German (G.)[1]:—

a	*as in*	man (German)	nama (*name*).
á	,,	father	stán (*stone*).
æ	,,	man	glæd (*glad*).
ǽ			dǽd (*deed*).
e	,,	été (F.)	ic ete[2] (*I eat*).

[1] Where no key-word is given for a long vowel, it must be pronounced exactly like the corresponding short one, only lengthened.

[2] Both vowels.

é	*as in*	see (G.)	hé (*he*).
ę	„	men	męnn (*men*).
i	„	fini (F.)	cwic (*alive*).
í	„	sieh (G.)	wín (*wine*).
ie	„	fin	ieldran (*ancestors*).
íe			híeran (*hear*).
o	„	beau (F.)	god (*god*).
ó	„	so (G.)	gód (*good*).
u	„	sou (F.)	sunu (*son*).
ú	„	gut (G.)	nú (*now*).
y	„	véc*u* (F.)	synn (*sin*).
ý	„	grün (G.)	brýd (*bride*).
ea	=	æ + a	eall (*all*).
éa	=	ǽ + a	éast (*east*).
eo	=	e + o	weorc (*work*).
éo	=	é + o	déop (*deep*).

The diphthongs are pronounced with the stress on the first element.

Those who find a difficulty in learning strange vowel-sounds may adopt the following approximate pronunciation:—

a	*as in*	ask (short)	nama (năhmăh).
á	„	father	stán (stahn).
æ	„	man	glæd (glad).
ǽ	„	th*e*re	ǽr (air).
e, ę	„	men	ete (etty), męnn (men).
é	„	th*ey*	hé (hay).
i, ie	„	fin	cwic (quick), ieldran (ildrăhn).
í, íe	„	see	wín (ween), híeran (heerăhn).
o	„	not	god (god).
ó	„	note	gód (goad).
u	„	full	full (full).
ú	„	fool	nú (noo).
y	„	fin	synn (zin).
ý	„	see	brýd (breed).

ea	=	ĕ-ăh	eall (ĕ-ăhl).
éa	=	ai-ăh	éast (ai-ăhst).
eo	=	ĕ-o	weorc (wĕ-ork).
éo	=	ai-o	déop (dai-op).

The pronunciation given in parentheses is the nearest that can be expressed in English letters as pronounced in Southern English.

CONSONANTS.

Double consonants must be pronounced double, or long, as in Italian. Thus *sunu* (son) must be distinguished from *sunne* (sun) in the same way as *penny* is distinguished from *penknife*. So also *in* (in) must be distinguished from *inn* (house); noting that in English final consonants in accented monosyllables after a short vowel are long, our *in* and *inn* both having the pronunciation of Old English *inn*, not of O. E. *in*.

c was hard before all vowels, as in *cirice* (chirch), *cyning* (king), and was pronounced before *n*, as in *cnoll* (summit), *cnáwan* (know).

g was always sounded in *ng*, as in *engel* (angel,=enggel), *lang* (long). Before *i*, *e* single *g* had the sound of our *y*:—*gif* (if,=yiv), *ic lufige* (I love,=luviye), *ged'ón* (done), *gé* (ye), *giefan* (give,=yivan), *geard* (yard), *géong* (young). In *licgan* (lie), *hrycg* (back), &c. *cg* represented a sound nearly equivalent to *gg*.

f had the sound of *v* everywhere where it was possible:—*faran* (go), *of* (of), *ofer* (over); not, of course, in *oft* (often), or when doubled, as in *offrian* (offer).

h initially, as in *hé* (he), had the same sound as now. Everywhere else it had that of Scotch and German *ch* in *loch*:—*héah* (high), *Wealh* (Welshman), *riht* (right). *hw*, as in *hwæt* (what), *hwíl* (while), had the sound of our *wh*; and *hl*, *hn*, *hr* differed from *l*, *n*, *r* respectively precisely as *wh* differs from *w*, that is, they were these consonants devocalized, *hl* being nearly the same as Welsh *ll* :—*hláford* (lord), *hlúd* (loud); *hnappian* (doze), *hnutu* (nut); *hraþe* (quickly), *hréod* (reed).

r was always a strong trill, as in Scotch :—*rǽran* (to raise), *hér* (here), *word* (word).

s had the sound of *z* :—*sécan* (seek), *swá* (so), *wís* (wise), *ár·ísan* (rise); not, of course, in combination with hard consonants, as in *stán* (stone), *fæst* (firm), *ricsian* (rule), or when double, as in *cyssan* (kiss).

þ had the sound of our *th* (=dh) in *then* :—*þú* (thou), *þing* (thing), *sóþ* (true), *hǽþen* (heathen); except when in combination with hard consonants, where it had that of our *th* in *thin*, as in *sécþ* (seeks). Note *hæfþ* (has)=*hævdh*.

w was fully pronounced wherever written :—*wrítan* (write), *niwe* (new), *séow* (sowed *pret.*).

STRESS.

The stress or accent is marked throughout in this book, whenever it is not on the first syllable of a word, by (·) following the letter on which the stress begins. Thus *forg·iefan* is pronounced with the same stress as that of *forgive*, *and·swaru* with that of *answer*.

PHONOLOGY.

VOWELS.

Different vowels are related to one another in various ways in O. E., the most important of which are mutation and gradation.

The following changes are *mutations* :—

a .. **ę** :—mann, *pl.* męnn; wand (wound *prt.*), węndan (to turn).

á .. **ǽ** :—bláwan (to blow), blǽwþ (bloweth); hál (sound), hǽlan (heal).

u .. **y** :—burg (city), *pl.* byrig; trum (strong), trymman (to strengthen).

o .. **y** :—gold, gylden (golden); coss (a kiss), cyssan (to kiss).

e .. **i** :—beran (to bear), bireþ (beareth); cweþan (speak), cwide (speech).

u .. **o** :—curon (they chose), gecoren (chosen).

ú .. **ý** :—cúþ (known), cýþan (to make known); fúl (foul), áfýlan (defile).

ó .. **é** :—sóhte (sought *prt.*), sécan (to seek); fóda (food), fédan (to feed).

éa .. **íe** :—héawan (to hew), híewþ (heweth); téam (progeny), tíeman (teem).

éo .. **íe** :—stéor (rudder), stíeran (steer); gestréon (possession), gestríenan (gain).

Before proceeding to gradation, it will be desirable to describe the other most important vowel-relations.

a, æ, ea. In O. E. original *a* is preserved before nasals, as in *mann*, *lang*, *nama* (name), and before a single consonant followed by *a*, *u* or *o*, as in *dagas* (days), *dagum* (to days), *faran* (go), *gafol* (profit), and in some words when *e* follows, as in *ic fare* (I go), *faren* (gone). Before *r*, *l*, *h* followed by another consonant, and before *x* it becomes *ea*, as in *heard* (hard), *eall* (all), *eald* (old), *eahta* (eight), *weaxan* (to grow). In most other cases it becomes *æ*:—*dæg* (day), *dæges* (of a day), *fæst* (firm), *wær* (wary).

e before nasals always becomes *i*: compare *bindan* (to bind), pret. *band*, with *beran* (to bear), pret. *bær* (æ=a).

e before *r* (generally followed by a consonant) becomes *eo*:—*eorþe* (earth), *heorte* (heart). Also in other cases:—*ṣeolfor* (silver), *heofon* (heaven).

i before *r* + cons. becomes *ie*:—*bierþ* (beareth) contr. from *bireþ*, *hierde* (shepherd) from *heord* (herd), *wiersa* (worse).

ę before *r*, or *l* + cons. often becomes *ie*:—*fierd* (army) from *faran*, *bieldo* (boldness) from *beald*, *ieldra* (elder) from *eald*.

By *gradation* the vowels are related as follows:—

e (i, eo) . . **a** (æ, ea) . . **o** (u):—

bindan (inf.), *band* (pret.), *bundon* (they bound); *beran* (inf.), *bær* (pret.), *boren* (past partic.); *ceorfan* (cut), *cearf* (pret.), *curfon* (they cut), *corfen* (past partic.). *bęnd* (bond) = mutation of *band*, *byr-þen* (burden) of *bor-en*.

a (æ, ea) . . **ǽ**:—*spræc* (spoke), *sprǽcon* (they spoke), *sprǽc* (speech).

a . . **ó**:—*faran* (to go), *fór* (pret.), *fór* (journey). *gef·éra* (companion) mutation of *fór*.

í . . **á** . . **i**:—*wrítan*, *wrát*, *writon*. *gew·rit* (writing, *subst.*). (*be*)*l·ífan* (*sb.* remain), *láf* (remains), whence by mutation *lǽfan* (leave).

éo (ú) . . **éa** . . **u** (o):—*céosan* (choose), *céas*, *curon*, *coren*. *cys-t* (choice). (*for*)*l·éosan* (lose), *léas* (loose), *ál·íesan* (release), *losian* (to be lost). *búgan* (bend), *boga* (bow).

We see that the laws of gradation are most clearly shown in the conjugation of the strong verbs. But they run through the whole language, and a knowledge of the laws of gradation and mutation is the main key to O. E. etymology.

It is often necessary to supply intermediate stages in connecting two words. Thus *lęcgan* (lay) cannot be directly referred to *licgan* (lie), but only to a form **lag-*, preserved in the preterite *læg*. So also *blęndan* (to blind) can be referred only indirectly to the adjective *blind* through an intermediate **bland-*. Again the root-vowel *byrþen* (burden) cannot be explained by the infinitive *beran* (bear), but only by the past participle *geb·oren*. In the same way *hryre* (fall *sb.*) must be referred, not to the infinitive *hréosan*, but to the preterite plural *hruron* or past participle *geh·roren*.

CONSONANTS.

s becomes *r* in the preterite plurals and past participles of strong verbs, as in *curon*, *gec·oren* from *céosan*, *wǣron*, pl. of *wæs* (was), and in other formations, such as *hryre* (fall) from *hréosan*.

þ becomes *d* under the same conditions, as in *wurdon*, *gew·orden* from *weorþan* (become), *cwæþ* (quoth), pl. *cwǣdon*, *cwide* (speech) from *cweþan* (infin.).

r is often transposed, as in *iernan* (run) from original **rinnan* (cp. the subst. *ryne*), *berstan* (burst) from **brestan*, *hors* (horse) from **hross*.

The combinations **cæ-**, **gæ-** become *cea-*, *gea-*, as in *ceaf* (chaff) from **cæf*, *geaf* (gave) = **gæf* from *giefan* (cp. *cwæþ* from *cweþan*), *geat* (gate), pl. *gatu*—cp. *fæt* (vessel), pl. *fatu*.

gǣ- often becomes *géa-*, as in *géafon* (they gave), with which compare *cwæþ*, *cwǣdon*.

ge- regularly becomes *gie-*, as in *giefan*, *gieldan* (pay) from **gefan*, **geldan*—cp. *cweþan*, *delfan*.

When **g** comes before a consonant in inflection, it often becomes *h*, as in *hé líehþ* (he lies) from *léogan* (mentiri).

h after a consonant is dropt when a vowel follows, thus *Wealh* (Welshman) has plural *Wealas*.

INFLECTIONS.

NOUNS.

Gender. There are three genders in O. E.—masculine,

neuter, and feminine. The gender is partly natural, partly grammatical. By the natural gender names of male beings, such as *se mann* (the man), are masculine; of female beings, such as *séo dohtor* (the daughter), are feminine; and of young creatures, such as *þæt cild* (the child), neuter. Note, however, that *þæt wíf* (woman) is neuter.

Grammatical gender is known only by the gender of the article and other words connected with the noun, and, to some extent, by its form. Thus all nouns ending in *-a*, such as *se móna* (moon), are masculine, *séo sunne* (sun) being feminine. Those ending in *-dóm*, *-hád*, and *-scipe* are also masculine:—*se wísdóm* (wisdom), *se cildhád* (childhood), *se fréondscipe* (friendship). Those in *-nes*, *-o* (from adjectives), and *-ung* are feminine:—*séo rihtwísnes* (righteousness), *séobieldo* (boldness) from *beald*, *séo scotung* (shooting).

Compounds follow the gender of their last element, as in *þæt burg-geat* (city-gate), from *séo burg* and *þæt geat*. Hence also *se wíf-mann* (woman) is masculine.

The gender of most words can be learnt only by practice, and the student should learn each noun with its proper definite article.

Strong and Weak. Weak nouns are those which form their inflections with *n*, such as *se móna*, plural *mónan*; *séo sunne*, genitive sing. *þǽre sunnan*. All the others, such as *se dæg*, pl. *dagas*, *þæt hús* (house), gen. sing. *þæs húses*, are strong.

Cases. There are four cases, nominative, accusative, dative, and genitive. The acc. is the same as the nom. in all plurals, in the sing. of all neuter nouns, and of all strong masculines. Masculine and neuter nouns never differ in the plural except in the nom. and acc., and in the singular they differ only in the acc. of weak nouns, which in neuters is the same as the nom. The dative plural of nearly all nouns ends in *-um*.

STRONG MASCULINES.

(1) as-plurals.

SINGULAR.		PLURAL.	
Nom[1].	stán (*stone*).	*Nom.*	stán-as.
Dat.	stán-e.	*Dat.*	stán-um.
Gen.	stán-es.	*Gen.*	stán-a.

So also *dǽl* (part), *cyning* (king), *cildhád* (childhood).

dæg (day) changes its vowel in the pl. (p. 5):—*dæg*, *dæge*, *dæges*; *dagas*, *dagum*, *daga*.

Nouns in *-e* have nom. and dat. sing. the same:—*ęnde* (end), *ęnde*, *ęndes*; *ęndas*, *ęndum*, *ęnda*.

Nouns in *-el*, *-ol*, *-um*, *-en*, *-on*, *-er*, *-or* often contract:—*ęngel* (angel), *ęngle*, *ęngles*; *ęnglas*, *ęnglum*, *ęngla*. So also *nægel* (nail), *þegen* (thane), *ealdor* (prince). Others, such as *æcer* (field), do not contract.

h after a consonant is dropped in inflection (p. 7), as in *feorh* (life), *feore*, *feores*. So also in *Wealh* (Welshman), plur. *Wealas*.

There are other classes which are represented only by a few nouns each.

(2) e-plurals.

A few nouns which occur only in the plur.:—*léode* (people), *léodum*, *léoda*. So also several names of nations:—*Ęngle* (English), *Dęne* (Danes).

(3) Mutation-plurals.

SINGULAR.		PLURAL.	
Nom.	fót (*foot*).	*Nom.*	fét.
Dat.	fét.	*Dat.*	fót-um.
Gen.	fót-es.	*Gen.*	fót-a.

[1] Wherever the acc. is not given separately, it is the same as the nom.

So also *tóþ* (tooth). *Mann* (man), *męnn, mannes; męnn, mannum, manna.*

(4) u-nouns.

SINGULAR.		PLURAL.	
Nom.	sun-u (*son*).	*Nom.*	sun-a.
Dat.	sun-a.	*Dat.*	sun-um.
Gen.	sun-a.	*Gen.*	sun-a.

So also *wudu* (wood).

(5) r-nouns (including feminines).

SINGULAR.		PLURAL.	
Nom.	módor (*mother*).	*Nom.*	módor.
Dat.	méder.	*Dat.*	módr-um.
Gen.	módor.	*Gen.*	módr-a.

So also *bróþor* (brother), *dohtor* (daughter). *Fæder* (father) has dat. sing. *fæder.*

(6) nd-nouns.

Formed from the present participle of verbs.

SINGULAR.		PLURAL.	
Nom.	fréond (*friend*).	*Nom.*	friend.
Dat.	friend.	*Dat.*	fréond-um.
Gen.	fréond-es.	*Gen.*	fréond-a.

So also *féond* (enemy).

Those in *-end* inflect thus:—*búend* (dweller), *búend, búendes; búend, búendum, búenda.* So also *hǽlend* (saviour).

STRONG NEUTERS.

(1) u-plurals.

SINGULAR.		PLURAL.	
Nom.	scip (*ship*).	*Nom.*	scip-u.
Dat.	scip-e.	*Dat.*	scip-um.
Gen.	scip-es.	*Gen.*	scip-a.

So all neuters with short root-syllable, such as *geb·ed* (prayer), *gew·rit* (writing), *geat* (gate).

Fæt (vessel), *fæte*, *fætes* ; *fatu*, *fatum*, *fata*.

Ríce (kingdom), *ríce*, *ríces* ; *ríeu*, *rícum*, *ríca*. So also *geþéode* (language), *stycce* (piece).

Those in *-ol*, *-en*, *-or*, &c. are generally contracted :—*déofol* (devil), *déofles*, *déoflu*. So also *wǽpen* (weapon), *mynster* (monastery), *wundor* (wonder).

Cild (child) has plur. *cildru*, *cildrum*, *cildra*.

(2) Unchanged plurals.

SINGULAR.		PLURAL.	
Nom.	hús (*house*).	*Nom.*	hús.
Dat.	hús-e.	*Dat.*	hús-um.
Gen.	hús-es.	*Gen.*	hús-a.

So many other long monosyllables, such as *bearn* (child), *folc* (nation), *wíf* (woman).

Feoh (money) drops its *h* in inflection and lengthens the *eo* :—*feoh*, *féo*, *féos*. So also *bleoh* (colour).

STRONG FEMININES.

(1) a-plurals.

	SINGULAR.		PLURAL.	
(*a*)	*Nom.*	gief-u (*gift*).	*Nom.*	gief-a.
	Acc.	gief-e.		
	Dat.	gief-e.	*Dat.*	gief-um.
	Gen.	gief-e.	*Gen.*	gief-ena.

So also *lufu* (love), *scamu* (shame). *Duru* has in the sing. *duru*, *duru*, *dura*, *dura*, gen. pl. *dura*. Observe that all these nouns have a short root-syllable. When it is long, the *u* is dropped, and the noun falls under (*b*).

	SINGULAR.		PLURAL.	
(*b*)	*Nom.*	spræ̆c (*speech*).	*Nom.*	spræ̆c-a.
	Acc.	spræ̆c-e.		
	Dat.	spræ̆c-e.	*Dat.*	spræ̆c-um.
	Gen.	spræ̆c-e.	*Gen.*	spræ̆c-a.

So also *strǽt* (street), *sorg* (sorrow). Some have the acc. sing. the same as the nom., such as *dǽd, hand, miht.*

Those in *-ol*, *-er*, *-or*, &c. contract:—*sáwol* (soul), *sáwle, sáwla, sáwlum.* So also *ceaster* (city), *hlǽdder* (ladder).

Some in *-en* double the *n* in inflection:—*byrþen* (burden), *byrþenne.* So also those in *-rǽden,* such as *hierdrǽden* (guardianship).

(2) Mutation-plurals.

SINGULAR.		PLURAL.	
Nom.	bóc (*book*).	*Nom.*	béc.
Dat.	béc.	*Dat.*	bóc-um.
Gen.	béc.	*Gen.*	bóc-a.

Burg (city), *byrig, byrig; byrig, burgum, burga.*

(3) Indeclinable.

SINGULAR.	
Nom.	bieldo (*boldness*).
Dat.	bieldo.
Gen.	bieldo.

So also *ieldo* (age).

For *r*-nouns, see under Masculines.

WEAK MASCULINES.

SINGULAR.		PLURAL.	
Nom.	nam-a (*name*).	*Nom.*	nam-an.
Acc.	nam-an.		
Dat.	nam-an.	*Dat.*	nam-um.
Gen.	nam-an.	*Gen.*	nam-ena.

So also all nouns in *-a*:—*gef·éra* (companion), *guma* (man), *gel·éafa* (belief). *Ieldran* (elders) occurs only in the plural.

Gef·éa (joy) is contracted throughout:—*geféa*, *geféan*.

WEAK NEUTERS.

SINGULAR.		PLURAL.	
Nom.	éag-e (*eye*).	*Nom.*	éag-an.
Acc.	éag-e.		
Dat.	éag-an.	*Dat.*	éag-um.
Gen.	éag-an.	*Gen.*	éag-ena.

WEAK FEMININES.

SINGULAR.		PLURAL.	
Nom.	sunn-e (*sun*).	*Nom.*	sunn-an.
Acc.	sunn-an.		
Dat.	sunn-an.	*Dat.*	sunn-um.
Gen.	sunn-an.	*Gen.*	sunn-ena.

So also *cirice* (church), *fǽmne* (virgin).

Léo (lion) has acc., &c. *léon*.

PROPER NAMES.

Native names of persons are declined like other nouns:—*Ælfréd*, gen. *Ælfrédes*, dat. *Ælfréde*; *Éad-burg* (fem.), gen. *Éadburge*, &c.

Foreign names of persons sometimes follow the analogy of native names, thus *Crist*, *Salomon* have gen. *Cristes*, *Salomones*, dat. *Criste*, *Salomone*. Sometimes they are declined as in Latin, especially those in *-us*, but often with a mixture of English endings, and the Latin endings are used somewhat loosely, the accus. ending being often extended to the other oblique cases; thus we find nom. *Cyrus*, gen. *Cyres*, acc. *Cyrum*, dat. *Cyrum* (þám cyninge Cyrum).

Almost the only names of countries and districts in Old English are those taken from Latin, such as *Breten* (Britain), *Cęnt* (Kent), *Germania* (Germany), and those formed by composition, generally with *land*, such as *Ęngla-land* (land of the English, England), *Israhela-þéod* (Israel). In both of these cases the first element is in the gen. pl., but ordinary compounds, such as *Scot-land*, also occur. In other cases the name of the inhabitants of a country is used for the country itself:—*on Éast-ęnglum*=in East-anglia, lit. 'among the East-anglians.' So also *on Angel-cynne*=in England, lit. 'among the English race,' more accurately expressed by *Angelcynnes land.*

Uncompounded names of countries are sometimes undeclined. Thus we find *on Cęnt.*

Germania, *Asia*, and other foreign names in *-a* take *-e* in the oblique cases, thus gen. *Germanie.*

ADJECTIVES.

Adjectives have three genders, and the same cases as nouns, though with partly different endings, together with strong and weak inflection. In the masc. and neut. sing. they have an *instrumental* case, for which in the fem. and plur. the dative is used.

STRONG ADJECTIVES.

Adjectives with a short root-syllable take *-u* in the *fem. sing. nom.* and *neut. pl. nom.*, those with a long one drop it.

SINGULAR.

	Masc.	Neut.	Fem.
(*a*) *Nom.*	cwic (*alive*),	cwic,	cwic-u.
Acc.	cwic-ne,	cwic,	cwic-e.
Dat.	cwic-um,	cwic-um,	cwic-re.
Gen.	cwic-es,	cwic-es,	cwic-re.
Instr.	cwic-e,	cwic-e.	

PLURAL.

Nom.	cwic-e,	cwic-u,	cwic-e.
Dat.		cwic-um.	
Gen.		cwic-ra.	

So also *sum* (some), *fǽrlic* (dangerous).

Those with *æ*, such as *glæd* (glad), change it to *a* in dat. *gladum*, &c.

Those in *-e*, such as *blíþe* (glad), drop it in all inflections:—*blíþne, blíþu, blíþre.*

Those in *-ig, -el, -ol, -en, -er, -or* often contract before inflections beginning with a vowel, as in *hálig* (holy), *hálges, hálgum; micel* (great), *miclu, micle.* Not, of course, before consonants:—*háligne, micelne, micelra.*

Those in *-u*, such as *gearu* (ready), change the *u* into a *w* before vowels:—*gearwes, gearwe.*

Adjectives with long root-syllable drop the *u* of the short-syllable ones:—

	Masc.	Neut.	Fem.
(*b*) *Nom. Sing.*	gód (*good*),	gód,	gód.
Plur.	góde,	gód,	góde.

Féa (few) has only the plural inflections, dat. *féam*, gen. *féara.*

Héah (high) drops its second *h* in inflection and contracts:—*héare*, nom. pl. *héa*, dat. *héam*, acc. sing. masc. *héanne.*

Fela (many) is indeclinable.

WEAK ADJECTIVES.

The weak inflections of adjectives agree exactly with the noun ones :—

SINGULAR.

	Masc.	Neut.	Fem.
Nom.	gód-a,	gód-e,	gód-e.
Acc.	gód-an,	gód-e,	gód-an.
Dat.	gód-an,	gód-an,	gód-an.
Gen.	gód-an,	gód-an,	gód-an.

PLURAL.

Nom.	gód-an.
Dat.	gód-um.
Gen.	gód-ena.

The vowel- and consonant-changes are as in the strong declension.

COMPARISON.

The comparative is formed by adding *-ra*, and is declined like a weak adjective :—*léof* (dear), *léofra* masc., *léofre* fem., *léofran* plur., etc.; *mǽre* (famous), *mǽrra*. The superlative is formed by adding *-ost*, and may be either weak or strong :—*léofost* (dearest).

The following form their comparisons with mutation, with superlative in *-est* (the forms in parentheses are adverbs) :—

eald (*old*),	ieldra,	ieldest.
lang (*long*),	lęngra,	lęngest.
néah (*near*),	(néar),	níehst.

The following show different roots :—

gód (*good*),	bętera,	bętst.
yfel (*evil*),	wiersa,	wierrest.
micel (*great*),	mára (má),	mǽst.
lytel (*little*).	læssa (læs),	læst.

The following are defective as well as irregular, being formed from adverbs :—

ǽr (*formerly*),	ǽrra (ǽror),	ǽrest.
fore (*before*),	. . .	forma, fyrmest.
út (*out*),	ýterra,	ýtemest.

NUMERALS.

CARDINAL.		ORDINAL.
án,	*one.*	forma (*first*).
twá,	*two.*	óþer.
þréo,	*three.*	þridda.
féower,	*four.*	féorþa.
fíf,	*five.*	fíf-ta.
siex,	*six.*	siex-ta.
seofon,	*seven.*	seofoþa.
eahta,	*eight.*	eahtoþa.
nigon,	*nine.*	nigoþa.
tíen,	*ten.*	téoþa.
ęndlufon,	*eleven.*	ęndlyf-ta.
twęlf,	*twelve.*	twęlf-ta.
þréo-tíene,	*thirteen.*	þréo-téoþa.
féower-tíene,	*fourteen.*	
fíf-tíene,	*fifteen.*	
siex-tíene,	*sixteen.*	
seofon-tíene,	*seventeen.*	
eahta-tíene,	*eighteen.*	
nigon-tíene,	*nineteen.*	
twęn-tig,	*twenty.*	
þri-tig,	*thirty.*	
féower-tig,	*forty.*	
fíf-tig,	*fifty.*	
siex-tig,	*sixty.*	

CARDINAL.

hund-s·eofon-tig,	*seventy.*
hund-e·ahta-tig,	*eighty.*
hund-n·igon-tig,	*ninety.*
hund, hundred, hund-t·éontig,	*hundred.*
hund-ę·ndlufontig,	*hundred and ten.*
hund-t·węlftig,	*hundred and twenty.*
þúsend,	*thousand.*

Án is declined like other adjectives.

Twá is declined thus:—

	Masc.	Neut.	Fem.
Nom.	twegen,	twá,	twá.
Dat.		twám.	
Gen.		twegra.	

So also *begen* (both), *bá*, *bám*, *begra*.

þréo is declined thus:—

	Masc.	Neut.	Fem.
Nom.	þríe,	þréo,	þréo.
Dat.		þrim.	
Gen.		þréora.	

The others up to *twęntig* are generally indeclinable. Those in *-tig* are sometimes declined like neuter nouns, sometimes like adjectives, and are often left undeclined. When not made into adjectives they govern the genitive.

Hund and *þúsend* are either declined as neuters or left undeclined, always taking a genitive:—*eahta hund míla* (eight hundred miles), *féower þúsend wera* (four thousand men).

Units are always put before tens:—*án and twentig* (twenty-one).

The ordinals are always weak, except *ōþer*, which is always strong.

PRONOUNS.

PERSONAL.

SINGULAR.

Nom.	ic (*I*),	þú (*thou*).
Acc.	mé,	þé.
Dat.	mé,	þé.
Gen.	mín,	þín.

DUAL.

Nom.	wit (*we two*),	git (*ye two*).
Acc.	unc,	inc.
Dat.	unc,	inc.
Gen.	uncer,	incer.

PLURAL.

Nom.	wé (*we*),	gé (*ye*).
Acc.	ús,	éow.
Dat.	ús,	éow.
Gen.	úre,	éower.

SINGULAR.

	Masc.	Neut.	Fem.
Nom.	hé (*he*),	hit (*it*),	héo (*she*).
Acc.	hine,	hit,	híe.
Dat.	him,	him,	hiere.
Gen.	his,	his,	hiere.

PLURAL.

Nom.	híe (*they*).
Dat.	him.
Gen.	hiera.

There are no reflexive pronouns in O. E., and the ordinary

personal pronouns are used instead:—*híe ges·amnodon híe* (they collected themselves, assembled); *híe áb·ǽdon him wíf* (they asked for wives for themselves). *Self* is used as an emphatic reflexive adjective agreeing with its pronoun:—*swá swá híe wýscton him selfum* (as they wished for themselves).

POSSESSIVE.

Mín (my), *þín* (thy), *úre* (our), *éower* (your), and the dual *uncer* and *incer* are declined like other adjectives. The genitives *his* (his, its), *hiere* (her), *hiera* (their) are used as indeclinable possessives.

INTERROGATIVE.

	Masc. and Fem.	Neut.
Nom.	hwá (*who*),	hwæt (*what*).
Acc.	hwone,	hwæt.
Dat.	hwám,	hwám.
Gen.	hwæs,	hwæs.
Instr.	hwý,	hwý.

Hwelc (which) is declined like a strong adjective: it is used both as a noun and an adjective.

DEMONSTRATIVE.

SINGULAR.

	Masc.	Neut.	Fem.
Nom.	se (*that, the*),	þæt,	séo.
Acc.	þone,	þæt,	þá.
Dat.	þám,	þám,	þǽre.
Gen.	þæs,	þæs,	þǽre.
Instr.	þý,	þý,	. . .

PLURAL.

Nom.	þá.
Dat.	þám.
Gen.	þára.

Se is both a demonstrative and a definite article. It is also used as a personal pronoun:—*hé geh·ierþ mín word, and wyrcþ þá* (he hears my words, and does them). *Sé* as a demonstrative and pers. pronoun has its vowel long.

SINGULAR.

	Masc.	Neut.	Fem.
Nom.	þes (*this*),	þis,	þéos.
Acc.	þisne,	þis,	þás.
Dat.	þissum,	þissum,	þissere.
Gen.	þisses,	þisses,	þissere.
Instr.	þýs,	þýs,	. . .

PLURAL.

Nom.	þás.
Dat.	þissum.
Gen.	þissera.

Other demonstratives, which are used both as nouns and as adjectives, are *se ilca* (same), which is always weak, *swelc* (such), which is always strong.

RELATIVE.

The regular relative is the indeclinable *þe*, as in *ǽlc þára þe þás mín word geh·ierþ* (each of those who hears these my words). It is often combined with *se*, which is declined:—*se þe*=who, masc., *séo þe*, fem., &c. *Se* alone is also used as a relative:—*hér is mín cnapa, þone ic gec·éas* (here is my servant, whom I have chosen); sometimes in the sense of 'he who':—*hér þú hæfst þæt þín is* (here thou hast that which is thine).

INDEFINITE.

Indefinites are formed with *swá* and the interrogative pronouns, thus:—*swá hwá swá, swá hwelc swá* (whoever), *swá hwæt swá* (whatever).

Án and *sum* (some) are used in an indefinite sense:—*án mann*, *sum mann*=‘a certain man,’ hence ‘a man.’ But the indefinite article is generally not expressed.

Ǽlc (each), *ǽnig* (any), *nǽnig* (no, none), are declined like other adjectives.

Óþer (other) is always strong:—*þá óþre mẹnn.*

Man, another form of *mann*, is often used in the indefinite sense of ‘one,’ French *on*:—*his bróþor Horsan man ofs·lóg* (they killed his brother Horsa).

VERBS.

There are two classes of verbs in O. E., *strong* and *weak.* The conjugation of strong verbs is effected mainly by means of vowel-mutation, that of weak verbs by the addition of *d* (-ode, -de) to the root-syllable.

The following is the conjugation of the strong verb *bindan* (bind), which will serve to show the endings which are common to all verbs:—

		INDICATIVE.	SUBJUNCTIVE.
Pres. sing.	1.	bind-e,	bind-e.
	2.	bind-est, bintst,	bind-e.
	3.	bind-eþ, bint,	bind-e.
plur.		bind-aþ,	bind-en.
Pret. sing.	1.	band,	bund-e.
	2.	bund-e,	bund-e.
	3.	band,	bund-e.
plur.		bund-on,	bund-en.

Imper. sing. bind; *plur.* bind-aþ. *Infin.* bind-an.
Partic. pres. bind-endė; *pret.* ge-b·und-en.
Gerund. tó bind-enne.

For the plural *bindaþ*, both indicative and imperative, *binde* is used when the personal pronoun follows immediately after the verb:—*wé bindaþ* (we bind), but *binde wé* (let us bind); so also *gáþ !* (go plur.), but *gá gé !* (go ye).

The present participle may be declined like an adjective. Its declension when used as a noun is given above, p. 10.

The past participle generally prefixes *ge-*, as in *geb·unden*, *gen·umen* from *niman* (take), unless the other parts of the verbs have it already, as in *geh·ieran* (hear), *geh·iered.* No *ge* is added if the verb has another prefix, such as *á-*, *be-*, *for-*; thus *forg·iefan* (forgive) has the past participle *forg·iefen.* It may be declined like an adjective.

Traces of an older passive voice are preserved in the form *hát-te* from *hátan* (call, name), which is both present 'is called,' and preterite 'was called';—*se munuc hátte Abbo* (the monk's name was Abbo).

STRONG VERBS.

In the strong verbs the plural of the pret. indic. generally has a different vowel from that of the sing. (*ic band*, *wé bundon*). The 2nd sing. pret. indic. and the whole pret. subj. always have the vowel of the preterite plural indicative (*þú bunde*, *ic bunde*, *wé bunden*).

The 1st and 2nd persons sing. of the pres. indic. often mutate the root-vowel, thus:—

a	*becomes*	ę	*as in*	(hé) stęnt	*from*	standan (*stand*).
ea	„	ie	„	fielþ	„	feallan (*fall*).
e	„	i	„	cwiþþ	„	cweþan (*say*).
eo	„	ie	„	wierþ	„	weorþan (*happen*).
á	„	ǽ	„	hǽtt	„	hátan (*command*).
ó	„	é	„	gréwþ	„	grówan (*grow*).
éa	„	íe	„	híewþ	„	héawan (*hew*).
éo	„	íe	„	cíest	„	céosan (*choose*).

The full ending of the 3rd pers. sing. pres. indic. is *-eþ*, which is generally contracted, with the following consonant-changes:—

-teþ	*becomes*	-tt	*as in*	lǽtt	*from*	lǽtan (*let*).
-deþ	„	-tt	„	bítt	„	bídan (*wait*).
-ddeþ	„	-tt	„	bitt	„	biddan (*pray*).
-þeþ	„	-þþ	„	cwiþþ	„	cweþan (*say*).
-seþ	„	-st	„	cíest	„	céosan (*choose*).
-ndeþ	„	-nt	„	bint	„	bindan (*bind*).

Double consonants become single, as in *hé fielþ* from *feallan*.

Before the *-st* of the 2nd pers. consonants are often dropt, as in *þú cwist* from *cweþan*, *þú cíest* from *céosan*; and *d* becomes *t*, as in *þú bintst* from *bindan*.

For the changes between *s* and *r*, *þ* and *d*, *g* and *h*, see p. 7.

Some verbs, such as *séon* (see), dropt the *h* and contract before most inflections beginning with a vowel:—*ic séo*, *wé séoþ*, *tó séonne*; but *hé sihþ*.

There are seven conjugations of strong verbs, distinguished mainly by the different formation of their preterites. The following lists comprise all the strong verbs that occur in the texts given in this book, together with several others of the commoner ones.

I. 'Fall'-conjugation.

The pret. sing. and pl. has *éo* or *é*, and the past partic. retains the original vowel of the infinitive.

(*a*) *éo-preterites.*

ea :—

INFINITIVE.	THIRD PRES.	PRET. SING.	PRET. PL.	PARTIC. PRET.
feallan (*fall*)	fielþ	féoll	féollon	feallen
healdan (*hold*)	hielt	héold	héoldon	healden
wealdan (*wield*)	wielt	wéold	wéoldon	wealden
weaxan (*grow*)	wixt	wéox	wéoxon	weaxen

á :—

bláwan (*blow*)	blǽwþ	bléow	bléowon	bláwen
cnáwan (*know*)	cnǽwþ	cnéow	cnéowon	cnáwen
sáwan (*sow*)	sǽwþ	séow	séowon	sáwen

é :—

wépan (*weep*)	wépþ	wéop	wéopon	wópen

Wépan has really a weak present (p. 30) with mutation (the original *ó* re-appearing in the past partic.), but it makes no difference in the inflection. *Fón* and *hón* originally had *a* in the infin. and present.

ó :—

flówan (*flow*)	fléwþ	fléow	fléowon	flówen
grówan (*grow*)	gréwþ	gréow	gréowon	grówen
rówan (*row*)	réwþ	réow	réowon	rówen

éa :—

béatan (*beat*)	bíett	béot	béoton	béaten
héawan (*hew*)	híewþ	héow	héowon	héawen
hléapan (*leap*)	hlíepþ	hléop	hléopon	hléapen

(*b*) *é-preterites.*

á :—

hátan (*command*)	hǽtt	hét	héton	háten

ó :—

fón (*seize*)	féhþ	féng	féngon	fangen
hón (*hang*)	héhþ	héng	héngon	hangen

II. 'Shake'-conjugation.

Verbs in *a* (*ea*) and *ę* (*ie*). *Ó* in pret. sing. and pl., *a* (*æ*) in partic. pret. *Standan* drops its *n* in the pret. The partic. pret. of *swęrian* is irregular.

a:—

INFINITIVE.	THIRD PRES.	PRET. SING.	PRET. PL.	PARTIC. PRET.
faran (*go*)	færþ	fór	fóron	faren
sacan (*quarrel*)	sæcþ	sóc	sócon	sacen
standan (*stand*)	stęnt	stód	stódon	standen

The following shows contraction of original *ea*:—

sléan (*strike*)	slihþ	slóg	slógon	slægen

ę:—

hębban (*lift*)	hęfþ	hóf	hófon	hafen
sciеppan (*create*)	sciepþ	scóp	scópon	scapen
swęrian (*swear*)	swęreþ	swór	swóron	sworen

The presents of these verbs are inflected weak, so that their imperative sing. is *hęfe* and *swęre*, like that of *węnian* (p. 32). *Swęrian* has indic. *swęrige*, *swęrest*, like *węnian*; *hębban* has *hębbe*, *hęfst*, &c. like *hieran* (p. 30).

III. 'Bind'-conjugation.

I (*ie*, *e*, *eo*) followed by two consonants, one or both of which is nearly always a liquid (*l*, *r*) or nasal (*m*, *n*), in the infin., *a* (*æ*, *ea*) in pret. sing., *u* in pret. pl., *u* (*o*) in ptc. pret. *Findan* has a weak preterite.

i:—

bindan (*bind*)	bint	band	bundon	bunden
drincan (*drink*)	drincþ	dranc	druncon	druncen
findan (*find*)	fint	funde	fundon	funden
gieldan (*pay*)	gielt	geald	guldon	golden
(on)ginnan (*begin*)	-ginþ	-gann	-gunnon	-gunnen
grindan (*grind*)	grint	grand	grundon	grunden

INFINITIVE.	THIRD PRES.	PRET. SING.	PRET. PL.	PARTIC. PRET.
iernan (*run*)	iernþ	arn	urnon	urnen
ge-l·impan (*happen*)	-limpþ	-lamp	-lumpon	-lumpen
scrincan (*shrink*)	scrincþ	scranc	scruncon	scruncen
springan (*spring*)	springþ	sprang	sprungon	sprungen
swincan (*toil*)	swincþ	swanc	swuncon	swuncen
windan (*wind*)	wint	wand	wundon	wunden
winnan (*fight*)	winþ	wann	wunnon	wunnen
e :—				
berstan (*burst*)	bierst	bærst	burston	borsten
bregdan (*pull*)	. . .	brægd	brugdon	brogden
delfan (*dig*)	dilfþ	dealf	dulfon	dolfen
sweltan (*die*)	swilt	swealt	swulton	swolten
eo :—				
beorgan (*protect*)	bierhþ	bearg	burgon	borgen
beornan (*burn*)	biernþ	barn	burnon	burnen
ceorfan (*cut*)	cierfþ	cearf	curfon	corfen
feohtan (*fight*)	fieht	feaht	fuhton	fohten
weorpan (*throw*)	wierpþ	wearp	wurpon	worpen
weorþan (*become*)	wierþ	wearþ	wurdon	worden

IV. 'Bear'-conjugation.

Verbs in *e* (*i*), followed by a single consonant, generally a liquid or nasal; in *brecan* the liquid precedes the vowel. *A* (*æ*) in pret. sing., *ǽ* (*á*) in pret. pl., *o* (*u*) in ptc. pret. *Cuman* is irregular.

i :—				
niman (*take*)	nimþ	nam	námon	numen
e :—				
beran (*bear*)	bierþ	bær	bǽron	boren
brecan (*break*)	bricþ	bræc	brǽcon	brocen
sceran (*shear*)	scierþ	scær	scǽron	scoren
stelan (*steal*)	stilþ	stæl	stǽlon	stolen

u :—

INFINITIVE.	THIRD PRES.	PRET. SG.	PRET. PL.	PARTIC. PRET.
cuman (*come*)	cymþ	cóm	cómon	cumen

V. 'Give'-conjugation.

Verbs in *e* (*i*, *eo*, *ie*) followed by single consonants, which are not liquids or nasals. This class differs from the last only in the ptc. pret. which keeps the vowel of the infinitive.

e :—

cweþan (*say*)	cwiþþ	cwæþ	cwǽdon	cweden
etan (*eat*)	itt	æt	ǽton	eten
sprecan (*speak*)	spricþ	spræc	sprǽcon	sprecen
wrecan (*avenge*)	wricþ	wræc	wrǽcon	wrecen

i :—

biddan (*pray*)	bitt	bæd	bǽdon	beden
licgan (*lie*)	líþ	læg	lǽgon	legen
sittan (*sit*)	sitt	sæt	sǽton	seten
þicgan (*receive*)	þigeþ	þeah	þǽgon	þegen

All these have weak presents :—imper. *bide*, *lige*, *site*, *þige*. Their *i*'s are mutations of the *e* which appears in their past partic.

ie :—

giefan (*give*)	giefþ	geaf	géafon	giefen
(on)gietan (*understand*)	-giett	-geat	-géaton	-gieten

The following is contracted in most forms :—

séon (*see*)	sihþ	seah	sáwon	sewen

VI. 'Shine'-conjugation.

Verbs in *í*, with pret. sing. in *á*, pl. *i*, ptc. pret. *i*.

bídan (*wait*)	bítt	bád	bidon	biden
bítan (*bite*)	bítt	bát	biton	biten
drífan (*drive*)	drífþ	dráf	drifon	drifen

INFINITIVE.	THIRD PRES.	PRET. SING.	PRET. PL.	PARTIC. PRET.
(be)lífan (*remain*)	-lífþ	-láf	-lifon	-lifen
rídan (*ride*)	rítt	rád	ridon	riden
rípan (*reap*)	rípþ	ráp	ripon	ripen
(á)rísan (*rise*)	-ríst	-rás	-rison	-risen
scínan (*shine*)	scínþ	scán	scinon	scinen
sníþan (*cut*)	sníþþ	snáþ	snidon	sniden
stígan (*ascend*)	stígþ	stág	stigon	stigen
(be)swícan (*deceive*)	-swícþ	-swác	-swicon	-swicen
gew·ítan (*depart*)	-wítt	-wát	-witon	-witen
wrítan (*write*)	wrítt	wrát	writon	writen

VII. 'Choose'-conjugation.

Verbs in *éo* and *ú*, with pret. sing. *éa*, pl. *u*, ptc. prt. *o*. *Fléon* and *téon* contract.

béodan (*offer*)	bíett	béad	budon	boden
bréotan (*break*)	bríett	bréat	bruton	broten
céosan (*choose*)	cíest	céas	curon	coren
fléogan (*fly*)	flíehþ	fléag	flugon	flogen
fléon (*flee*)	flíehþ	fléah	flugon	flogen
fléotan (*float*)	flíett	fléat	fluton	floten
hréosan (*fall*)	hríest	hréas	hruron	hroren
hréowan (*rue*)	hríewþ	hréaw	hruwon	hrowen
forl·éosan (*lose*)	-líest	-léas	-luron	-loren
scéotan (*shoot*)	scíett	scéat	scuton	scoten
sméocan (*smoke*)	smíecþ	sméac	smucon	smocen
téon (*pull*)	tíehþ	téah	tugon	togen
ú :—				
brúcan (*enjoy*)	brýcþ	bréac	brucon	brocen
búgan (*bow*)	býhþ	béag	bugon	bogen
lúcan (*lock*)	lýcþ	léac	lucon	locen
lútan (*bow*)	lýtt	léat	luton	loten
scúfan (*push*)	scýfþ	scéaf	scufon	scofen

WEAK VERBS.

There are three conjugations of weak verbs—(1) in *-an*, pret. *-de* (*hieran*, *hierde*, 'hear'); (2) in *-ian*, pret. *-ede* (*węnian*, *węnede*, 'wean'); (3) in *-ian*, pret. *-ode* (*lufian*, *lufode*, 'love'). The verbs of the first two conjugations nearly all have a mutated vowel in the present and infinitive, which those of the third conjugation very seldom have.

I. *an*-verbs.

This class of weak verbs has the same endings as the strong verbs, except in the pret. and past partic., which are formed by adding *-de* and *-ed* respectively, with the following consonant changes.

-ndde	*becomes*	-nde	*as in*	sęnde	*from*	sęndan (*send*).
-llde	"	-lde	"	fylde	"	fyllan (*fill*).
-tde	"	-tte	"	métte	"	métan (*find*).
-pde	"	-pte	"	dypte	"	dyppan (*dip*).
-cte	"	-hte	"	tǽhte	"	tǽcan (*show*).

The past partic. are generally contracted in the same way:—*sęnd*, *métt*, *tǽht*, but some of them often retain the uncontracted forms:—*fylled*, *dypped*. When declined like adjectives they drop their *e* where practicable:—*fylled*, plur. *fylde*; *hiered*, *hierde*.

The 2nd and 3rd pres. sing. ind. are contracted as in the strong verbs.

(*a*) 'Hear'-*class*.

		INDICATIVE.	SUBJUNCTIVE.
Pres. sing.	1.	hier-e (*hear*),	hier-e.
	2.	hier-st,	hier-e.
	3.	hier-þ,	hier-e.
plur.		hier-aþ,	hier-en.

		INDICATIVE.	SUBJUNCTIVE.
Pret. sing.	1.	híer-de,	híer-de.
	2.	híer-dest,	híer-de.
	3.	híer-de,	híer-de.
plur.		híer-don,	híer-den.

Imper. sing. híer; *plur.* híer-aþ. *Infin.* híer-an.

Ptc. pres. híer-ende; *pret.* híer-ed.

Gerund tó híer-enne.

Further examples of this class are:—

INFINITIVE.	THIRD PRES.	PRET.	PARTIC. PRET.
cýþan (*make known*)	cýþþ	cýþde	cýþed
fyllan (*fill*)	fylþ	fylde	fylled
(néa)lǽcan (*approach*)	-lǽcþ	-lǽhte	-lǽht
lǽdan (*lead*)	lǽtt	lǽdde	lǽdd
lęcgan (*lay*)	lęgþ	lęgde	lęgd
gelíefan (*believe*)	-líefþ	-líefde	-líefed
nęmnan (*name*)	nęmneþ	nęmnde	nęmned
sęndan (*send*)	sęnt	sęnde	sęnd
sęttan (*set*)	sętt	sętte	sętt
sméan (*consider*)	sméaþ	sméade	sméad
tǽcan (*show*)	tǽcþ	tǽhte	tǽht
węndan (*turn*)	węnt	węnde	węnd

(*b*) 'Seek'-*class.*

In this class the mutated vowels lose their mutation in the preterite and past partic., besides undergoing other changes in some verbs.

Those in double consonants (and *cg*) simplify them in the contracted 2nd and 3rd sing. pres. indic.:—*sęlle, sęlst, sęlþ; sęcge, sęgst, sęgþ*; also in the imperative, which is formed as in Conj. II:—*sęle, sęge, byge*, &c.

ę :—

INFINITIVE.	THIRD PRES.	PRET.	PARTIC. PRET.
cwęllan (*kill*)	cwęlþ	cwealde	cweald
ręccan (*tell*)	ręcþ	reahte	reaht
sęcgan (*say*)	sęgþ	sægde	sægd
sęllan (*give*)	sęlþ	sealde	seald
węccan (*wake*)	węcþ	weahte	weaht
þęncan (*think*)	þęncþ	þóhte	þóhte
i :—			
bringan (*bring*)	bringþ	bróhte	bróht
y :—			
bycgan (*buy*)	bygþ	bohte	boht
þyncan (*appear*)	þyncþ	þúhte	þúht
wyrcan (*work*)	wyrcþ	worhte	worht
é :—			
récan (*care*)	récþ	róhte	róht
sécan (*seek*)	sécþ	sóhte	sóht

II. 'Wean'-*conjugation.*

		INDICATIVE.	SUBJUNCTIVE.
Pres. sing.	1.	węn-ige (*wean*),	węn-ige.
	2.	węn-est,	węn-ige.
	3.	węn-eþ,	węn-ige.
plur.		węn-iaþ,	węn-ien.
Pret. sing.	1.	węn-ede,	węn-ede.
	2.	węn-edest,	węn-ede.
	3.	węn-ede,	węn-ede.
plur.		węn-edon,	węn-eden.

Imper. węn-e, węn-iaþ. *Infin.* węn-ian.

Partic. pres. węn-iende ; *pret.* węn-ed.

Gerund. tó węn-ienne.

So are conjugated all weak verbs with a short mutated root syllable, such as *fęrian* (carry), *węrian* (defend), *geb'yrian* (befit). There are not many of them.

III. 'Love'-*conjugation.*

		INDICATIVE.	SUBJUNCTIVE.
Pres. sing.	1.	luf-ige (*love*),	luf-ige.
	2.	luf-ast,	luf-ige.
	3.	luf-aþ,	luf-ige.
plur.		luf-iaþ,	luf-igen.
Pret. sing.	1.	luf-ode,	luf-ode.
	2.	luf-odest,	luf-ode.
	3.	luf-ode,	luf-ode.
plur.		luf-odon,	luf-oden.

Imper. luf-a, luf-iaþ. *Infin.* luf-ian.

Partic. pres. luf-iende; *pret.* luf-od. *Gerund.* tó luf-ienne.

So also *áscian* (ask), *macian* (make), *weorþian* (honour), and many others.

Irregularities.

Some verbs are conjugated partly after I, partly after III. Such are *habban* (have) and *libban* (live).

Habban has pres. indic. *hæbbe, hæfst, hæfþ; habbaþ*, subj. *hæbbe, hæbben*, pret. *hæfde*, imper. *hafa, habbaþ*, particc. *habbende, hæfd.*

Libban has pres. *libbe, leofast, leofaþ; libbaþ*, subj. *libbe*, pret. *leofode*, imper. *leofa, libbaþ*, particc. *libbende, leofod.*

Fętian (fetch) has pret. *fętte.*

STRONG-WEAK VERBS.

The strong-weak verbs have for their presents old strong

preterites, from which new weak preterites are formed. Note the occasional second persons sing. in *t*.

		INDICATIVE.	SUBJUNCTIVE.
Pres. sing.	1.	wát (*know*),	wite.
	2.	wást,	wite.
	3.	wát,	wite.
plur.		witon,	witen.
Pret.		wiste.	

Imper. wite, witaþ. *Infin.* witan.

Partic. pres. witende; *pret.* witen.

The other most important weak-strong verbs are given below in the 1st and 2nd sing. pres. indic., in the plur. indic., in the pret., in the infin. and partic. pret. Of several the last two forms are doubtful, or do not exist.

Áh (*possess*), áge, ágon; áhte; ágen (*only as adjective*)[1].

Cann (*know*), canst, cunnon; cúþe; cunnan; cúþ (*only as adjective*).

Dearr (*dare*), durre, durron; dorste.

Gem·an (*remember*), -manst; -munde; -munan.

Mæg (*can*), miht, magon, mæge (*subj.*); mihte; mugan.

Mót (*may*), móst, móton; móste; mótan.

Sceal (*shall*), scealt, sculon, scyle (*subj.*); scolde; sculan.

Þearf (*need*), þurfon, þyrfe (*subj.*); þorfte; þurfan.

The present *willan* (will) was originally a subj. pret.:—

		INDICATIVE.	SUBJUNCTIVE.
Pres. sing.	1.	wile,	wile.
	2.	wilt,	wile.
	3.	wile,	wile.
plur.		willaþ,	wilen.
Pret.		wolde.	

---

[1] So also *náh* = *ne* (not) *áh*.

Similarly *nyllan* (will not):—

		INDICATIVE.	SUBJUNCTIVE.
Pres. sing.	1.	nyle,	nyle.
	2.	nylt,	nyle.
	3.	nyle,	nyle.
plur.		nyllaþ,	nylen.
Pret.		nolde.	

ANOMALOUS VERBS.

(1) Wesan (*be*).

		INDICATIVE.	SUBJUNCTIVE.
Pres. sing.	1.	éom; béo,	síe; béo.
	2.	eart; bist,	síe; béo.
	3.	is; biþ,	síe; béo.
plur.		sind; béoþ,	síen; béon.
Pret. sing.	1.	wæs,	wǽre.
	2.	wǽre,	wǽre.
	3.	wæs,	wǽre.
plur.		wǽron,	wǽren.

Imper. wes, wesaþ; béo, béoþ. *Infin.* wesan; béon.

Partic. pres. wesende.

The contracted negative forms are:—*neom, neart, nis; næs, nǽre, nǽron; nǽre, nǽren.*

(2) Dón (*do*).

		INDICATIVE.	SUBJUNCTIVE.
Pres. sing.	1.	dó,	dó.
	2.	dést,	dó.
	3.	déþ,	dó.
plur.		dóþ,	dón.
Pret.		dyde.	

Imper. dó, dóþ. *Infin.* dón.

Partic. pres. dónde; *pret.* ged·ón.

(3) Gán (*go*).

		INDICATIVE.	SUBJUNCTIVE.
Pres. sing.	1.	gá,	gá.
	2.	gǽst,	gá.
	3.	gǽþ,	gá.
plur.		gáþ,	gán.
Pret.		éode,	éode.

Imper. gá, gáþ. *Infin.* gán.
Partic. pres. gánde; *pret.* geg·án.

DERIVATION.

PREFIXES.

The following are the most important prefixes, some of which are *verbal*, being confined to verbs and words formed directly from them; some *nominal*, being confined to nouns and adjectives.

á- (1) originally 'forth,' 'away,' as in *ár·ísan*, 'rise forth,' 'arise'; *áf·aran*, 'go away,' 'depart'; but generally only intensitive, as in *ác·węllan* (kill), *áh·réosan* (fall).

(2)='ever' in pronouns and particles, where it gives an indefinite sense, as in *á-hwǽr* (anywhere), *áwiht* (anything).

ǽg- from *á-ge-*, the *á* being mutated and the *e* dropped, has a similar meaning, as in *ǽg-hwelc* (each), *ǽgþer*=*ǽg-hwæþer* (either, *prn.*).

be- originally 'by,' 'around' (cp. the preposition *be*), (1) specializes the meaning of a transitive verb, as in *bes·ęttan* (beset, surround), *besc·ieran* (shear); (2) makes an intransitive verb transitive, as in *beþ·ęncan* (consider) from *þęncan* (think); (3) gives a privative meaning, as in *beh·éafdian* (behead). In some words, such as *bec·uman* (come), it is practically unmeaning.

for- (which is distinct from the preposition *for*) generally has the sense of 'loss' or 'destruction,' as in *ford·ón* (destroy), *forw·eorþan* (perish). Of course, if the verb with which it is compounded already has this meaning, it acts merely as an intensitive, as in *forb·réotan* (break up, break), *fors·crincan* (shrink up). It also modifies in a bad sense generally, as in *fors·éon* (despise), or negatives, as in *forb·éodan* (forbid).

ge- originally meant 'together,' as in *gef·éra* (fellow-traveller, companion) from *féran* (travel). With verbs it often signifies 'completion,' 'attainment,' and hence 'success,' as in *geg·án* (conquer), originally 'go over' or 'reach,' *gew·innan* (win) from *winnan* (fight). Hence generally prefixed to *híeran* and *séon*, *geh·íeran* and *ges·éon* strictly meaning 'succeed in hearing, seeing.' It is generally prefixed to past participles (p. 23), where it originally gave the meaning of completion—*gel·ufod*='completely loved.'

mis-='mis,' as in *mis-dǽd* (misdeed).

n-=*ne* (not), as in *ná* (not), literally 'never,' *nǽfre* (never), *næs* (was not)=*ne wæs*.

on- as a verbal prefix has nothing to do with the preposition *on*. It properly signifies 'separation,' as in *onl·úcan* (open) from *lúcan* (lock, close), but is often practically unmeaning, as in *ong·innan* (begin).

or-, literally 'out of,' is privative, as in *orsorg* (unconcerned) from *sorg* (sorrow).

tó- as a verbal prefix has nothing to do with the preposition *tó* (which occurs in *tóg·ædre*, 'together,' &c.), but signifies 'separation,' as in *tób·erstan* (burst asunder), *tób·regdan* (shake off), and hence 'destruction, as in *tóc·wíesan* (crush to pieces, bruise).

un- negatives, as in *un-gesǽlig* (unhappy).

D

ENDINGS.

(*a*) Nouns.

Personal.

-end, from the present participle *-ende,*='-er':—*hǽlend* (healer, Saviour), *búend* (dweller).

-ere='-er':—*sáwere* (sower), *mynetere* (money-changer, minter) from *mynet* (coin).

-ing, patronymic, *æþeling* (son of a noble, prince) from *æþele* (noble).

Abstract.

-nes, fem. from adjectives:—*gód-nes* (goodness), *rihtwís-nes* (righteousness).

-uþ, -þo, fem., generally from adjectives:—*géoguþ* (youth), *strengþo* (strength) from *strang.*

-ung, fem. from verbs:—*scotung* (shooting, shot), *hergung* (ravaging), from *scotian, hergian.*

The following are also independent words:—

-dóm, masc.:—*wís-dóm* (wisdom), *þéow-dóm* (servitude).

-hád, masc.:—*cild-hád* (childhood).

-rǽden, fem.:—*gecwid-rǽden* (agreement) from *cwide* (speech); *mann-rǽden* (allegiance).

-scipe, masc.:—*fréond-scipe* (friendship). Concrete in *wæter-scipe* (piece of water, water).

(*b*) Adjectives.

-en, with mutation, denotes 'material,' 'belonging to':—*gylden* (golden), *stǽnen* (of stone), *hǽþen* (heathen) from *hǽþ* (heath). In *seolcen* (silken) there is no mutation.

-feald='-fold':—*hund-feald* (hundred-fold).

-ig:—*miht-ig* (mighty); *hál-ig* (holy) from *hál* (whole).

-isc, with mutation:—*Englisc* (English) from *Angel*; *menn-isc* (human) from *mann*.

-ol:—*swic-ol* (deceitful).

-iht, with mutation, denotes 'material,' 'nature':—*stǽn-iht* (stony).

-sum='-some':—*híer-sum* (obedient).

The following exist (sometimes in a different form) as independent words:—

-fæst:—*sóþ-fæst* (truthful).

-full:—*sorg-full* (sorrowful), *gel·éaf-full* (believing, pious).

-léas='-less':—*ár-léas* (dishonoured, wicked).

-lic (cp. *gel·íc*) = '-ly':—*folc-lic* (popular), *heofon-lic* (heavenly).

-weard='-ward':—*súþan-weard* (southward).

Verbs.

-læ̂can:—*án-læ̂can* (unite), *geþ·wǽr-læ̂can* (agree).

Adverbs.

-e, the regular adverb-termination:—*lange* (long), *gel·íce* (similarly) from *lang*, *gel·íc*. Sometimes *-lice* (from *-lic*) is used to form adverbs, as *blíþe-lice* (gladly) from *blíþe*.

DERIVATIONS FROM PARTICIPLES.

Many abstract words are formed from present participles (often in a passive sense) and past participles (often in an active sense):—

-nes:—*forg·iefen-nes* (forgiveness), *ger·ecced-nes* (narrative), *welwillend-nes* (benevolence).

-lic:—*unárímed-lic* (innumerable).

-lice:—*welwillend-lice* (benevolently).

SYNTAX.

Gender.

When masculine and feminine beings are referred to by the same adjective or pronoun, the adjective or pronoun is put in the neuter :—*híe ges·amnodon híe, ealle þá héafod-mę̄nn, and éac swelce wíf-menn . . and þá híe blíþost wǣron . .* (they gathered themselves, all the chief men, and also women . . and when they were most merry . .). Here *blíþost* is in the neuter plur.

Cases.

Accusative. Some verbs of asking (a question) and requesting, together with *lǣran* (teach), take two accusatives, one of the person, and another of the thing :—*híe hine ne dorston ǣnig þing áscian* (they durst not ask him anything); *wé magon éow rǣd gel·ǣran* (we can teach you a plan).

The accusative is used adverbially to express duration of time : *hwý́ stande gé hér ealne dæg ídle ?* (why stand ye here all the day idle ?)

Dative. The dative in Old E. is of two kinds, (1) the dative proper, and (2) the instrumental dative, interchanging with the regular instrumental. It is not always easy to separate the two.

(1) The dative proper usually designates personal relations, and is frequently used with verbs, together with an accusative (generally of the thing). The dative is also used with adjectives. It is used not only with verbs of *giving*, &c., as in *hé sealde ǣlcum ánne pę̄ning* (he gave each a penny); *addressing*, as in *ic éow sęcge* (I say to you), *hé þancode his Dryhtne* (he thanked his Lord); but also with many verbs of *benefiting, influencing*, &c., as in *ne dó ic þé nánne téonan* (I do thee no injury), *híe noldon him líefan* (they would not allow

them to do so); *þám rę́þum stierde* (restrained the cruel ones). Also in looser constructions, to denote the person indirectly affected, benefited, &c., as in *bycgaþ éow ele* (buy for yourselves oil). Note especially the following idiom: *híe ges·óhton Bretene Brettum tó fultume* (they came to Britain as a help to the Britains—to help them); *hé clipode Crist him tó fultume* (he called Christ to his help).

The dative is also used with adjectives of *nearness, likeness*, &c.:—*Éadmund cyning clipode ánne biscop þe him geh·ęndost wæs* (King Edmund summoned a bishop who was nearest at hand to him); *heofona ríce is gel·íc þám mangere þe sóhte þæt góde męregrot* (the kingdom of the heavens is like the merchant who sought the good pearl).

(2) The instrumental dative is used to denote the *instrument* and *manner* of an action: *hé geę·ndode yflum déaþe* (he ended with an evil death). Hence its use to form adverbs, as in *scéafmǽlum* (sheafwise). It also signifies time when:—*þrim géarum ǽr þám þe hé forþf·érde* (three years before he died), which is also expressed by the instrumental itself:—*séo wolde ęfsian ǽlce géare þone sanct* (she used to cut the saint's hair every year); *þý féorþan géare his ríces* (in the fourth year of his reign). A past participle with a noun in the instrumental dative is used like the ablative absolute in Latin: *Hubba bel·áf on Norþhymbra-lande, gew·unnenum sige mid wælhréownesse* (H. remained in Northumbria, victory having been won with cruelty).

Genitive. The genitive is often used in a partitive sense:—*his féonda sum* (one of his enemies); *hiera fíf wǽron dysige* (five of them were foolish). Hence it is regularly used with *fela*, as in *fela wundra* (many miracles); also with numerals when used as substantives (p. 18).

The genitive is often used like an accusative to denote the object of various emotions and mental states, such as *joy, desire, remembering*:—*híe þæs fægnodon swíþe* (they rejoiced at it greatly); *me léofre wǽre þæt ic on gef·eohte féolle wiþ þám þe mín folc móste hiera eardes brúcan* (it would be pleasanter to me to fall in fight that my people might enjoy (possess) their country); *ic þæs gew·ilnige* (I desire that); *gif hé his feores róhte* (if he cared about his life); *hé wæs þæs Hǽlendes gem·yndig* (he was mindful of—he remembered the Saviour).

Some of these verbs, such as *biddan* (ask), take an accusative of the person and a genitive of the thing:—*hé hine hláfes bitt* (he asks him for bread).

Verbs of *depriving, restraining*, &c., have the same construction:—*nis Angel-cynn bed·ǽled Dryhtnes hálgena* (England is not deprived of the Lord's saints).

Some verbs of *giving*, &c., take a genitive of the thing and a dative of the person:—*him wæs oft·ogen ǽlces fódan* (they were deprived of all food).

The genitive is often used to *define* an adjective or noun:—*þú eart wierþe slęges* (thou art worthy of death); *on þám géare þe Ælfréd æþeling án and twęntig géara wæs* (in the year when prince Alfred was twenty-one).

Concord.

Adjectives agree with their nouns not only when used attributively (góde męnn), but also when the adjective follows the noun, either predicatively or in apposition:—*þá męnn sind góde; hé ges·eah óþre ídle standan* (he saw others standing idle); *híe cómon mid langum scipum, ná manigum* (they came with long ships, not many).

Apposition.

In such expressions as 'the island of Britain,' the second noun is not put in the genitive, but the two are simply put in apposition, both being declined separately:—*Breten iegland, on Bretene (þám) ieglande.* In 'king Alfred,' &c., the proper name is put first in the same way:—*Ælfréd æþeling* (prince Alfred); *on Æþelrédes cyninges dæge* (in the days of king Æþelred).

There is a similar apposition with the adjective *sum* followed by a noun or pronoun, as in *sume þá męnn* (some of the men); *þá þá hé séow, sumu híe féollon wiþ weg* (while he sowed, some of them [the seeds] fell by the road). Sometimes the pronoun precedes, as in *þá bǽdon híe sume þæt Samson móste him macian sum gamen* (then some of them asked that Samson might make some sport for them).

Another kind of apposition occurs in instances like the following, where we have an adjective agreeing with a following noun, and denoting a part of it:—*híe ges·ǽton súþanwearde Bretene ǽrest* (they occupied the south of Britain first); *súþanweard hit* (=þæt land) *hæfdon Peohtas* (the Picts had the south part of it).

ADJECTIVES.

The weak forms are used:

(1) after the definite article:—*se æþela cyning* (the noble king); *þæs æþelan cyninges, þæt góde męregrot, þá gódan męregrotu.*

(2) after *þis*:—*þás earman landléode* (these poor people, *pl.*); *þes hálga cyning* (this holy king), *þisses hálgan cyninges.*

(3) occasionally after other demonstrative and indefinite adjectives, and often after possessive pronouns:—*þíne dieglan gold-hordas* (thy hidden treasures).

(4) in the vocative:—*þú yfla þéow and sláwa!* (thou bad and slothful servant); *éalá þú léofa cyning!* (oh, thou dear king).

Note that *óþer* always keeps the strong form: *þá óþru díor* (the other wild beasts). So also do the possessive pronouns:

þás mín word (these my words). *Án* in the sense of 'one' keeps the strong form to distinguish it from the weak *ána*= 'alone': *þæt án déorwierþe męregrot* (the one precious pearl).

ARTICLES.

The definite article is omitted as in Modern English before names such as *God*, and also before *Dryhten* (the Lord), *Déofol* (the Devil), and names of nations:—*Bretta cyning* (king of the Britons).

It is omitted in many prepositional combinations, not only in those where it is omitted in Modern English also, as in *sigefæst on sǽ and on lande* (victorious on sea and on land), but also in many others: *gew·ęnde tó wuda ongéan* (went back to the wood); *se flothęre férde ęft tó scipe* (the army of pirates went back to their ships); *hé féng tó ríce* (he took the government—came to the throne).

The definite article is, on the other hand, sometimes used where it would not be in Modern E., as in *se mann*='man' (men in general).

The indefinite article is often not expressed at all:—*þæt dyde unhold mann* (an enemy did that); *hé bes·tealcode on land swá swá wulf* (he stole to land like a wolf). Or it is expressed by *sum*: *on þǽm lande wæs sum mann, Léofríc geh·áten* (in that country was a man called L.). Or by *án*, as in Modern English:—*án wulf wearþ ás·ęnd to bew·ęrienne þæt héafod wiþ þá óþru déor* (a wolf was sent to protect the head against the other wild beasts).

PRONOUNS.

Hwæt is used interrogatively of persons where we should use 'who':—*hé nyste hwæt híe wǽron* (he did not know who they were).

VERBS.

Number.

After *ǽlc þára þe* (each of-those-who) the verb is put in the sing., agreeing not with *þára þe* but with *ǽlc*:—*ǽlc þára þe þás mín word geh·ierþ* (each of those who hear these my words).

When *þæt* or *þis* is connected with a plural predicate by means of the verb 'to be,' the verb is put in the plural:—*þæt wǽron þá ǽrestan scipu Dęniscra manna þe Angel-cynnes land ges·óhton* (those were the first ships of Danish men which came to the land of the English race).

Impersonal verbs take an accusative of the person, sometimes also with a genitive of the thing.

Others, such as *þyncan* (appear), take a dative of the person:—*wæs him geþ·úht þæt híe beh·ýdden þæt héafod* (they thought they (the Danes) had hidden the head).

Tenses.

There being no future inflection in Old E., the present is used instead:—*ne áb·ýhþ nǽfre Eádmund Hinguare* (Edmund will never submit to H.); *gá gé on minne wíngeard, and ic sęlle éow þæt riht biþ* (go ye into my vineyard, and I will give you what is right). As we see in this example, there is a tendency to use *béon* in a future sense. Another example is *gif ic béo geb·unden mid seofum rápum, sóna ic béo gew·ield* (if I am bound with seven ropes, I shall at once be overcome). The future is sometimes expressed by *will* and *shall*, as in Modern English, though generally with a sense of volition with the one, and of necessity with the other, the idea of simple futurity coming out most clearly in the preterites *wolde* and *scolde*:—

Hé gel·ǽhte áne léon þe hine áb·ítan wolde (he seized a lion that was going to devour him); *híe wéndon þæt híe scolden máre onf·ón* (they expected to receive more).

The preterite has the meaning of the modern

(1) Preterite and imperfect:—*se sáwere ut éode his sǽd tó sáwenne, and þá þá hé séow* . . (the sower *went* out to sow his seed, and while he *was sowing* . .).

(2) Perfect:—*hér is mín cnapa, þone ic gec·éas* (here is my servant, whom I have chosen);—*úre cyning cóm nú hér tó lande* (our king has just landed here).

(3) Pluperfect:—*þá þá gec·ómon þe ymb þá ęndlyftan tíd cómon* (when those came who had come at the eleventh hour).

Periphrastic tenses are sometimes formed, as in Modern E., by *hæbbe* and *hæfde* with the past participles, and often have the meanings of the modern perfect and pluperfect respectively, as in *nú ic hæbbe gestríened óþru twá pund* (now I have gained two other pounds), but even the pluperfect often has the sense of a simple preterite. The participle is undeclinable in the later language, but originally it was declined, being really an adjective in apposition to the noun or pronoun governed by *habban*: *híe hæfdon hiera cyning áw·orpenne* (they had deposed their king).

The pluperfect sense is often indicated by the addition of the adverb *ǽr* (before):—*his sweora, þe ǽr wæs fors·lægen* (his neck, which had been cut through).

The periphrastic forms of intransitive verbs are formed with *wesan*:—*siþþan híe áf·arene wǽron* (after they had gone away). Here the participle always agrees with the noun or pronoun with which it is connected.

The periphrases with the present participle have no distinctive meanings of duration, &c.:—*án mann wæs eardiende on Israhela þéode, Manue geh·áten* (a man dwelt in Israel called Manne).

Passive.

The passive is formed with *wesan* or *weorþan* with the past participle. These forms are very vague in meaning, and the distinction between the two auxiliaries is not clearly marked, but *wesan* appears to indicate a state, *weorþan* an action.

wearþ gel·ufod is generally preterite or perfect in meaning: *án wulf wearþ ás·ęnd* (a wolf was sent); *míne léofe þegnas, þe on hiera będdum wurdon ofs·lægene* (my beloved thanes, who have been killed in their beds).

wæs gel·ufod, indicating a state, is naturally pluperfect in meaning:—*se ǽrendraca sægde his hláforde hú him gea·ndwyrd wæs* (the messenger told his lord how he had been answered).

Subjunctive.

The subjunctive states something not as a fact, as in the indicative, but merely as an object of thought. Hence it is used to express wish, conditions, doubt, &c.

A. In principal sentences.

Wish and *command* (often nearly equivalent to the imperative):—*þæs him sie wuldor and lof á bútan ęnde* (therefore let there be to him praise and glory ever without end); *ne hé ealu ne drince nǽfre oþþe wín* (nor shall he ever drink ale or wine).

B. In dependent sentences.

The chief cases are the following:—

(1) In *indirect narrative* and *question: séo cwén sægde þæt hiere nǽre be healfum dǽle ges·ægd be Salomones mǽrþo* (the queen said that she had not been told about Solomon's glory by half); *ic áscige hwǽr séo offrung sie* (I ask where the offering is); *męnn woldon scéawian hú hé lǽge* (men

wished to see how he lay). When the statement in the indirect narration is perfectly certain in itself, and not merely accepted on the authority of the speaker, it is put in the indicative:—*hé hiere sǽde on hwám his miht wæs* (he told her what his strength consisted in).

(2) After verbs of *desiring* and *commanding:*—

þæs ic gew·ilnige and gew·ýsce mid móde þæt ic ána ne bel·ífe æfter mínum léofum þegnum (that I desire and wish with heart that I may not remain alone after my dear thanes).

(3) To express *purpose:*—*þý læs gé þone hwǽte áwyrtwalien* (lest ye root up the wheat);—*Dryhten ást·ág niþer, tó þám þæt hé ges·áwe þá burg* (the Lord descended, in order that he might see the city).

(4) To express *result:*—*þú næfst þá mihte þæt þú mæge him wiþstandan* (thou hast not the power that thou canst withstand him).

(5) To express *hypothetical comparison* (as if):—*se wulf folgode forþ mid þǽm héafde, swelce hé tam wǽre* (the wolf followed on with the head, as if he were tame); *hé gel·ǽhte áne léon, and tób·rægd híe tó styccum, swelce hé tót·ǽre ticcen* (he seized a lion and tore her to pieces, as if he were rending a kid).

(6) In *conditional* clauses, generally with *gif* or *bútan*, and in *concessive* clauses with *þéah, þéah þe:*—*God wát þæt ic nyle áb·úgan fram his bíggengum ǽfre, swelte ic, libbe ic* (God knows that I will not swerve from his worship ever, whether I die or live); *þás flotmenn cumaþ, and þé cwicne geb·indaþ, bútan þú mid fléame þínum feore geb·eorge* (these pirates will come and bind thee alive, unless thou savest thy life with flight); *God hielt Éadmund hálne his líchaman óþ þone miclan dæg, þéah þe hé on moldan cóme* (God will keep Edmund

with his body whole until the great day, although he has come to earth—been buried). Sometime the idea of 'if' must be got from the context:—*clipiaþ tó þissum gieſtum swá hwelce swá gé gem·étén* (summon to this wedding whomsoever ye meet,=*if* ye meet any one); *híe beh·éton hiere sceattas wiþ þám þe héo bes·wice Samson* (they promised her money in consideration of her betraying Samson,=if she would..).

When the statement is assumed as unreal, instead of merely hypothetical, as in the above instances, both clauses are put in the subjunctive, the preterite being substituted for the present, as in Modern English also, where *if I were*.. implies *I am not*.. The modern distinction between *if I were* and *if I had been*, the former corresponding to the present indicative *I am not*, the latter to the preterite *I was not*, is not made in Old English, which uses *gif ic wǽre* in both instances. Sometimes the 'if'-clause has to be supplied in thought:—*mé léofre wǽre þæt ic ongef·eohte féolle wiþ þám þe mín folc móste hiera eardes brúcan* (I would rather fall in fight that my people might possess their country), where we must supply some such clause as *gif hit swá béon mihte* (if it might be so—if it were possible to save my people from conquest by my death).

(7) In clauses dependant on a *negative sentence*:—*nis nán þing þe his mihte wiþst·ande* (there is nothing that resists his might). Sometimes the negation must be gathered from the context, as in *se hálga is mǽrra þonne menn mægen ás·méan* (the saint is more illustrious than men can conceive= the saint is so illustrious that no men can conceive it).

(8) In other cases, to express uncertainty, futurity, &c.: *þín ríce gew·ît fram þé, óþ þæt þú wite þæt God gew·ielt manna ríca* (thy kingdom shall depart from thee, till thou knowest that God rules the kingdoms of men); *uton weor-*

þian úrne naman, ǽr þám þe wé síen tód·ǽlde geond ealle eorþan! (let us make our name famous, before we are dispersed over the earth).

The preterite subjunctive is often expressed by *should* and *would* with an infinitive, as in Modern English.

Scolde is used after verbs of *desiring, requesting* and *commanding*:—*biddende þone Ælm·ihtigan þæt hé him árian scolde* (praying the Almighty to have mercy on him). In the following example the verb of commanding is understood from the noun *ǽrende*:—*hé sęnde tó þám cyninge béotlic ǽrende, þæt hé áb·úgan scolde tó his mannrǽdenne, gif hé his feores róhte* (he sent to the king an arrogant message, that he was to turn to his allegiance, if he cared about his life).

Wolde is used after verbs of *purpose*:—*se cyning éode inn þæt he wolde ges·éon þá þe þǽr sǽton* (the king went in to see those who were sitting there).

Infinitive.

After verbs of commanding the infinitive often has a passive sense:—*híe héton him sęndan máran fultum* (they ordered that more forces should be sent to them). So also after verbs of hearing, &c.:—*þæt mǽste wæl þe wé sęcgan híerdon* (the greatest slaughter we have heard told of).

Gerund.

The gerund is used—

(1) to express purpose:—*út éode se sáwere his sǽd tó sáwenne* (the sower went forth to sow his seed).

(2) it defines or determines an adjective (adverb or noun): *hit is scandlic ymb swelc tó sprecenne* (it is shameful to speak of such things).

PREPOSITIONS.

Some prepositions govern the accusative, such as *þurh* (through), *ymbe* (about); some the dative (and instrumental), such as *æfter* (after), *ǽr* (before), *æt* (at), *be* (by), *binnan* (within), *bútan* (without), *for* (for), *fram* (from), *of* (of), *tó* (to).

Some govern both accusative and dative, such as *ofer* (over), *on* (on, in), *under* (under). The general rule is that when motion is implied they take the accusative, when rest is implied, the dative. Thus *on* with the accusative signifies 'into,' with the dative 'in.' But this rule is not strictly followed, and we often find the accusative used with verbs of rest, as in *hé his hús getimbrode ofer stán* (he built his house on a rock), and conversely, the dative with verbs of motion, as in *híe féollon on stǽnihte* (they fell on stony ground).

As regards the use and meaning of the prepositions, it must be noticed that *in* is very seldom used, its place being supplied by *on*, the meaning 'on' being in its turn often expressed by *ofer*, as in the passage just quoted.

When a thing is referred to, *þǽr* is substituted for *hit*, the preposition being joined on to the *þǽr*, so that, for instance, *þǽrtó* corresponds to *tó him*; *híe lǽddon þone cyning to ánum tréowe, and tíegdon hine þǽrtó* (they led the king to a tree, and tied him to it). So also *hérbeéastan* is equivalent to 'east of this (country).'

Prepositions sometimes follow, instead of preceding the word they modify, sometimes with other words intervening: *híe scuton mid gafelocum him tó* (they shot at him with missiles); *híe cwǽdon him betwéonan* (they said among themselves); *þám Ælmihtigan to lofe, þe híe on gelíefdon* (to the praise of the Almighty, in whom they believed), where *on* refers to the indeclinable *þe.* So also in *þæt hús þe hé inne wunode* (the house he dwelt in).

Where the noun modified by such a preposition is not expressed, the preposition becomes an adverb: *se cyning sęnde his hęre tó, and ford·yde þá mannslagan* (the king sent his army to the place, and destroyed the murderers).

Negation.

The negative particle is *ne,* which drops its *e* before some common verbs and pronouns, as in *nis=ne is, nán=ne án.* The negative particle is prefixed to every finite verb in a sentence, and to all the words besides which admit the contracted forms:—*tóc·wiesed hréod hé ne forb·riett* (he breaks not the bruised reed), *hit ná ne féoll* (it did not fall); *nán mann nyste nán þing* (no man knew anything). So also with *ne . . ne*=‘neither . . nor:’ *ne flitt hé ne hé ne hriemþ* (he neither disputes nor cries out).

Correlation.

Correlation is often more fully expressed in Old than in Modern English, as in *þá þá męnn slépon, þá cóm his féonda sum*=‘*when* the men slept, *then* came one of his enemies.’ In *þá þá*=‘when’ the two correlatives are brought immediately together:—*þá þá hé séow, sumu híe féollon wiþ weg*=‘then when he sowed, some of them fell by the road.’ In the following example the conjunction *þæt* is correlative with the pronoun *þæt*:—*þæs ic gew·ilnige þæt ic ána ne bel·ife æfter mínum léofum þegnum*—‘that I desire, that I may not remain alone after my dear thanes.’ Sometimes a word is used to include both the demonstrative and the relative meaning:—*hé geb·róhte hine þǽr hé hine ǽr gen·am* (he brought him to the place where he took him from).

Word-Order.

The Old English word-order resembles that of German in many respects, though it is not so strict, thus:—

The verb comes before its nominative when the sentence is headed by an adverb or adverbial group, or when the object or predicate is put at the head of the sentence:—*þá cwæþ se cyning* (then said the king); *ǽrest wǽron búend þisses landes Brettas* (at first the Britons were the inhabitants of this country); *on his dagum cómon ǽrest þréo scipu* (in his days three ships first came); *þæt bǽron olfendas* (camels carried it); *mǽre is se God þe Daniel on bel·iefþ* (great is the God that Daniel believes in).

The infinite often comes at the end of the sentence:—

Wé magon éow rǽd gel·ǽran (we can teach you a plan).

The finite verb often comes at the end in dependant sentences, an auxiliary verb often coming after an infinitive or participle; *þæt wǽron þá ǽrestan scipu Dęniscra manna þe Angel-cynnes land ges·óhton* (those were the first ships of Danish men which came to the land of the English race); *þæt mǽste wæl þe wé sęcgan híerdon óþ þisne andweardan dæg* (the greatest slaughter that we have heard tell of up to this present day); *þæt híe þone Godes mann áb·ítan scolden* (in order that they should devour the man of God).

There is a tendency to put the verb at the end in principal sentences also, or, at least, to bring it near the end: *hiene man ofs·lóg* (they killed him); *híe þǽr sige námon* (they got the victory there).

TEXTS.

I.

SENTENCES.

Án on-ginn is ealra þinga, þæt is God æl-m·ihtig. Se gel·éafa þe biþ bútan gódum weorcum, sé is déad; þis sind þára apostola word. Ic éom gód hierde: se góda hierde sęlþ his ágen líf for his scéapum. Úre Ál·íesend is se góda hierde, and wé cristene męnn sind his scéap. Se móna his léoht ne sęlþ, and steorran of heofone feallaþ. Swá swá wæter ád·wǽscþ fýr, swá ád·wǽscþ séo ælmesse synna.

Ealle ges·ceafta, heofonas and ęnglas, sunnan and mónan, steorran and eorþan, eall níetenu and ealle fuglas, sǽ and ealle fiscas, God ges·cóp and gew·orhte on siex dagum; and on þám seofoþan dæge hé geę·ndode his weorc; and hé beh·éold þá eall his weorc þe hé gew·orhte, and híe wǽron eall swíþe gód. Hé férde geond manigu land, bodiende Godes gel·éafan. Hé forl·ét eall woruld-þing. Se cyning beb·éad þæt man scolde ofer eall Angel-cynn scipu wyrcan; and hiera wæs swá fela swá nǽfre ǽr ne wæs on nánes cyninges dæge. Se cyning hét ofs·léan ealle þá Dęniscan męnn þe on Angel-cynne wǽron.

Þá ne mihton híe him nán word and-swarian, ne nán mann ne dorste hine nán þing máre áscian. Híe fuhton on þá burg ealne dæg, and þóhton þæt híe híe scolden áb·recan. Se eorl gew·ęnde west tó Ír-lande, and wæs þǽr ealne þone winter. Æþelréd cyning and Ælfréd his bróþor fuhton wiþ ealne þone hęre on Æsces-dúne.

Se mann is éce on ánum dǽle, þæt is, on þǽre sáwle; héo ne geę·ndaþ nǽfre. Gif se biscop déþ be his ágnum willan, and wile bindan þone un-scyldigan, and þone scyldigan ál·íesan, þonne forl·íest hé þá miht þe him God forg·eaf. Þéod winþ ong·éan þéode, and ríce ong·éan ríce. Ealle męnn éow hatiaþ for mínum naman. Hé gew·orhte fela wundra binnan þám fierste þe hé biscop wæs. Hé geh·ǽlde sum wíf mid hálgum wætre. Se cyning wearþ ofs·lægen fram his ágnum folce. On þám ilcan géare wæs se micla hungor geond Angel-cynn. Se mæsse-préost áscaþ þæt cild, and cwiþþ: 'Wiþs·æcst þú déofle?" Þonne andwyrt se god-fæder, and cwiþþ: 'Ic wiþs·ace déofle.' God ælm·ihtiga, gem·iltsa mé syn-fullum! Æþelréd cyning cóm hám tó his ágenre þéode, and hé glædlice fram him eallum onf·angen wearþ.

Crist, úre Dryhten, beb·éad his leornung-cnihtum þæt híe scolden tǽcan eallum þéodum þá þing þá hé self him tǽhte. Gif gé forg·iefaþ mannum hiera synna, þonne forg·iefþ éower se heofonlica Fæder éowre synna. Ne mæg nán mann twám hláfordum þéowian: oþþe hé ánne hataþ and óþerne lufaþ, oþþe hé biþ ánum geh·íersum and óþrum ungehíersum.

Se cyning nam þæs eorles sunu mid him tó Ęnglą-lande. Męnn beh·ófiaþ gódre láre on þissum tíman, þe is geę·ndung þissere worulde. Se líchama, þe is þǽre sáwle réaf, andbídaþ þæs miclan dómes; and þéah hé béo tó dúste form·olsnod, God hine ár·ǽrþ, and geb·ringþ tóg·ædre sáwle and lícham an tó þám écan lífe. Hwelc fæder wile sęllan his cilde stán, gif hit hine hláfes bitt? Ág·iefaþ þám cásere þá þing þe þæs cáseres sind, and Gode þá þing þe Godes sind. Séo sáwol and-bídaþ þæs écan ǽristes.

Hé wæs cyning ofer eall Ęngla-land twęntig wintra. God ælm·ihtig is ealra cyninga cyning, and ealra hláforda hláford. Déofol is ealra un-riht-wísra manna héafod, and þá yflan męnn sind his limu. Synfulra manna déaþ is yfel and earmlic, for þám þe híe faraþ of þissum scortan lífe tó écum wítum. Hú fela hláfa hæbbe gé? Seofon, and féa fisca. Ne gew·ilna þú óþres mannes ǽhta!

On þám landum eardodon Ęngle, ǽr þám þe híe hider on land cómon. Híe fuhton on þá burg ealne dæg, ac híe ne mihton híe áb·recan. Þá éodon híe tó hiera scipum. Þǽr béoþ swíþe manige byrig on þám lande, and on ǽlcre byrig biþ cyning.

God cwæþ tó Noe: 'Ic wile ford·ón eall man-cynn mid wætre for hiera synnum, ac ic wile geh·ealdan þé, and þín wíf, and þíne þríe suna.' Án mann hæfde twegen suna; þá cwæþ hé tó þám ieldran: 'gá and wyrc tó-d·æg on mínum wín-gearde.' Þá cwæþ hé: 'ic nyle:' éode þéah siþþan tó þám wíngearde. Hé dyde his fæder willan. Se préost cwæþ tó þám folce: 'Ic éow blétsige on naman þæs Fæder, þæs Suna, and þæs Hálgan Gástes.' Ára þínum fæder and þínre méder! Sum wíf cóm to Criste, and bæd for hiere dehter. Séo dohtor wearþ geh·ǽled þurh gel·éafan þǽre méder.

Béoþ gem·yndige þára twegra worda þe Dryhten cwæþ on

his gód-spelle! Hé cwæþ: 'Forg·iefaþ, and éow biþ forg·iefen; sȩllaþ, and éow biþ ges·eald.'

Twegen mȩnn éodon intó Godes temple híe tó geb·iddenne. Ælfréd cyning fór mid þrim scipum út on sǽ, and gef·eaht wiþ féower scip-hlæstas Dȩniscra manna, and þára scipa twá gen·am, and þá mȩnn ofs·lægene wǽron þe þǽr-on wǽron. Þá cómon þréo scipu. Þá gef·éngon híe þára þréora scipa twá, and þá mȩnn ofs·lógon, ealle bútan fífum. Se wítega áw·rát be þám féower níetenum þe him ætí·ewdu wǽron, þæt híe hæfden éagan him on ǽlce healfe. Án þára níetena wæs on mȩnniscre onsíene him ætí·ewed, óþer on léon ansíene, þridde on cealfes, féorþe on earnes.

God þone ǽrestan mann rihtne and gódne ges·cóp, and eall man-cynn mid him. Ælfréd Æþelwulfing wæs cyning ofer eall Angel-cynn bútan þám dǽle þe under Dȩna onwealde wæs. Ǽlc gód tréow bierþ góde wæstmas, and ǽlc yfel tréow bierþ yfle wæstmas; ne mæg þæt góde tréow beran yfle wæstmas, ne þæt yfle tréow góde wæstmas. Éadigu sind éowru éagan, for þám þe híe ges·éoþ, and éowru éaran, for þám þe híe geh·íeraþ. Swá hwá swá sȩlþ ánum þurstigum manne ceald wæter on mínum naman, ne forl·íest hé his méde. Ne fare gé on hǽþenra manna wege! Gód mann of gódum gold-horde bringþ gód forþ; and yfel mann of yflum goldhorde bringþ yfel forþ.

Gregorius se hálga pápa is rihtlice gec·weden Ȩngliscre þéode apostol. Þá hé ges·eah þæt se mǽsta dǽl þǽre þéode his láre fors·áwon, þá forl·ét hé híe, and gec·éas þá hǽþnan léode. Gif se blinda blindne lǽtt, híe feallaþ begen on ánne pytt. Se Hálga Gást is lufu and willa þæs Fæder and þæs Suna; and híe sind ealle gel·íce mihtige. Bȩtere is séo sáwol þonne se mȩte, and bȩtera se líchama þonne his scrúd.

Séo sáwol is gást, and be eorþlicum męttum ne leofaþ. Beh·ealdaþ þás fléogandan fuglas, þe ne sáwaþ ne ne rípaþ, ac se heofonlica Fæder híe áf·étt. Hé cwæþ, 'Ic néom óþrum mannum gel·íc;' swelce hé cwǽde, 'Ic ána éom riht-wís, and þá óþre sind syn-fulle.'

Þá se Hǽlend þanon fór, þá folgodon him twegen blinde, cweþende: 'Gem·iltsa unc, Davides sunu!' Hé cwæþ tó him: 'Gel·íefe git þæt ic inc mæge geh·ǽlan?' Hé cwæþ: 'Síe inc æfter incrum gel·éafan.' Æþelstán cyning fór inn on Scot-land, ǽgþer ge mid land-hęre ge mid scip-hęre, and his micel ofer-h·ęrgode. Se mann þe God forg·iett, God forg·iett éac hine. Faraþ, and lǽraþ ealle þéoda! Lǽraþ híe þæt híe healden eall þá þing þe ic éow beb·éad! Sume męnn sǽdon be him þæt hé wǽre Ælfrédes sunu cyninges. Se Hǽlend áscode his leornung-cnihtas, 'Hwane sęcgaþ męnn þæt síe mannes Sunu?" Hwæt sęcge gé þæt ic síe? Þú eart þæs libbendan Godes sunu. Crist cwæþ be his Fæder: 'Gé sęcgaþ þæt hé éower God síe, and gé hine ne onc·néowon.' Gif híe þone hálgan Fæder onc·néowen, þonne underf·éngen híe mid gel·éafan his Sunu, þe hé á-s·ęnde tó middan-gearde. Se weg is swíþe nearu and sticol se þe lǽtt to heofona ríce; and se weg is swíþe brád and sméþe se þe lǽtt tó hęlle wíte. Dysig biþ se weg-férenda mann se þe nimþ þone sméþan weg þe hine mis-lǽtt, and forl·ǽtt þone sticolan þe hine geb·ringþ tó þǽre byrig. Þæt ic éow sęcge on þéostrum, sęcgaþ hit on léohte; and þæt gé on éare geh·íeraþ, bodiaþ uppan hrófum. Híe scufon út hiera scipu, and gew·ęndon him beg·eondan sǽ.

Healdaþ and dóþ swá hwæt swá híe secgaþ; and ne dó gé ná æfter hiera weorcum: híe sęcgaþ, and ne dóþ. Eall hiera weorc híe dóþ þæt męnn híe ges·éon. Híe lufiaþ þæt man híe gréte on strǽtum. Éalá gé nǽddran and nǽddrena cynn, hú fléo gé fram hęlle dóme?

Wé sind ealle cuman on þissum and-weardan lífe, and úre eard nis ná hér; ac wé sind hér swelce weg-férende męnn: án cymþ, óþer færþ. Hwelc mann sęlþ his bearne nǽddran, gif hit fisces bitt? Ǽlc þára þe bitt, hé onf·éhþ; and se þe sécþ, hé hit fint. Ne gǽþ ǽlc þára on heofona ríce þe cwiþþ tó mé, 'Dryhten, Dryhten;' ac se þe wyrcþ mínes Fæder willan þe on heofonum is, sé gǽþ on heofona ríce. Nis hit ná gód þæt man nime bearna hláf and hundum weorpe. Ic hæbbe þegnas under mé: and ic cweþe tó þissum, 'gá,' and hé gǽþ; and tó óþrum, 'cum,' and hé cymþ, and to mínum þéowe, 'wyrc þis,' and hé wyrcþ.

Se Hǽlend gen·am þá fíf hláfas, and blétsode, and tó-b·ræc, and tód·ǽlde bet·wix þám sittendum; swá gel·íce éac þá fiscas tód·ǽlde; and híe ealle gen·óh hæfdon. Þá þe þǽr ǽton wǽron féower þúsend manna, bútan cildrum and wífum. Híe cómon tó him, and tó him gebǽdon, and þus cwǽdon: 'Sóþlice þú eart Godes sunu.' Ne wéne gé þæt ic cóme sibbe on eorþan to sęndenne: ne cóm ic sibbe tó sęndenne, ac sweord. Hé beb·éad þæt híe sǽten ofer þǽre eorþan. Hé sǽde þæt Norþ-manna land wǽre swíþe lang and swíþe smæl.

Híe ealle on þone cyning wǽron feohtende, óþ þæt híe hine ofslægenne hæfdon. Ǽlc mann þe óþre męnn fors·ihþ biþ fram God fors·ewen. Se þe éaran hæbbe to geh·íerenne, geh·íere. Gód is ús hér tó béonne.

God cwæþ tó ánum wítegan, se wæs Ionas geh·áten: 'Far tó þǽre byrig, and boda þǽr þá word þe ic þé sęcge.'

Lufiaþ éowre fíend, and dóþ wel þám þe éow yfel dóþ. Lufa Dryhten þínne God on ealre þínre heortan, and on ealre þínre sáwle, and on eallum þínum móde. Se þe ne lufaþ his bróþor, þone þe hé ges·ihþ, hú mæg hé lufian God, þone þe hé ne ges·ihþ lícham-lice? Sęge ús hwanne þás þing gew·eorþen, and hwelc tácen síe þínes tó-cymes and worulde geę·ndunge.

Se Hǽlend cwæþ tó ánum his leornung-cnihta, se wæs háten Philippus: 'Mid hwám magon wé bycgan hláf þissum folce?' Wel wiste Crist hwæt hé dón wolde, and hé wiste þæt Philippus þæt nyste. God mæg dón eall þing; wé sculon wundrian his mihte, and éac gel·íefan. Crist ár·ǽrde Lazarum of déaþe, and cwæþ tó his leornung-cnihtum: 'Tó-l·íesaþ his bęndas, þæt hé gán mæge.' God is ælm·ihtig, and mæg dón eall þæt hé wile. Gé nyton on hwelcre tíde éower hláford ,cuman wile. For þám béo gé gearwe; for þám þe mannes Sunu wile cuman on þǽre tíde þe gé nyton. Se Hǽland cwæþ be his Fæder: 'Ic hine cann, and gif ic sęcge þæt ic hine ne cunne, þonne béo ic léas, éow gel·íc.'

Se déofol cwæþ tó Criste: 'Gif þú síe Godes sunu, cweþ tó þissum stánum þæt híe béon áw·ęnde tó hláfum.' Þá and-wyrde se Hǽlend, and cwæþ: 'Hit is áw·riten, "ne leofaþ se mann ná be hláfe ánum, ac leofaþ be eallum þám wordum þe gáþ of Godes múþe."' Se Hǽlend cóm tó him, þǽr híe wǽron geg·adrode, and cwæþ: 'Síe sibb bet·wix éow; ic hit éom; ne béo gé ná áf·yrhte.' Fæder úre, þú þe eart on heofonum, síe þín nama geh·álgod. Wé syngodon, wé dydon un-rihtlice; sęle ús forg·iefnesse: hwæt sculon wé dón?

II.

FROM THE GOSPEL OF ST. MATTHEW.

VII. 24–7.

Ǽlc þára þe þás mín word geh·íerþ, and þá wyrcþ, biþ gel·íc þám wísan were, se his hús ofer stán get·imbrode. Þá cóm þǽr regen and micel flód, and þǽr bléowon windas, and áh·ruron on þæt hús, and hit ná ne féoll: sóþlice hit wæs ofer stán get·imbrod.

And ǽlc þára þe geh·íerþ þás mín word, and þá ne wyrcþ, se biþ gel·íc þám dysigan męnn, þe get·imbrode his hús ofer sand-ceosol. Þá rínde hit, and þǽr cóm flód, and bléowon windas, and áh·ruron on þæt hús, and þæt hús féolḷ; and his hryre wæs micel.

XII. 18–21.

Hér is mín cnapa, þone ic gec·éas; mín gec·orena, on þám wel gelícode mínre sáwle: ic ás·ętte mínne gást ofer hine, and dóm hé bodaþ þéodum. Ne flítt hé, ne hé ne hríemþ, ne nán mann ne geh·íerþ his stefne on strǽtum. Tóc·wíesed hréod hé ne forb·ríett, and sméocende fleax hé ne ád·wǽscþ, ǽr þám þe hé áw·eorpe dóm tó sige. And on his naman þéoda geh·yhtaþ.

XIII. 3–8.

Sóþlice út éode se sáwere his sǽd tó sáweñne. Anḍ þá þá hé séow, sumu híe féollon wiþ weg, and fuglas cómon and ǽton þá. Sóþlice sumu féollon on stǽnihte, þǽr hit næfde micle eorþan, and hrædlice upp sprungon, for þám þe híe næfdon þǽre eorþan díepan; sóþlice, upp sprungenre sunnan, híe ád·rúgodon and fors·cruncon, for þám þe híe næfdon wyrtruman. Sóþlice sumu féollon on þornas, and þá þornas wéoxon, and forþ·rysmdon þá. Sumu sóþlice féollon on góde eorþan, and sealdon wæstm, sum hund-fealdne, sum siextig-fealdne, sum þritig-fealdne.

XIII. 24–30.

Heofona ríce is gew·orden þám męnn gel·íc þe séow gód sǽd on his æcere. Sóþlice, þá þá męnn slépon, þá cóm his féonda sum, and ofer-s·éow hit mid coccele on-m·iddan þám hwǽte, and férde þanon. Sóþlice, þá séo wyrt wéox, and þone wæstm bróhte, þá æté·owde se coccel hine. Þá éodon þæs hláfordes þéowas and cwǽdon: 'Hláford, hú, ne séowe þú gód sǽd on þínum æcere? hwanon hæfde hé coccel?' Þá cwæþ hé: 'Þæt dyde unhold mann.' Þá cwǽdon þá þéowas: 'Wilt þú, wé gáþ and gadriaþ híe?' Þá cwæþ hé: 'Nese: þý læs gé þone hwǽte áw·yrtwalien, þonne gé þone coccel gadriaþ. Lǽtaþ ǽgþer weaxan óþ ríp-tíman; and on þám ríptíman ic sęcge þám ríperum: "gadriaþ ǽrest þone coccel, and bindaþ scéaf-mǽlum tó forb·ærnenne; and gadriaþ þone hwǽte intó mínum bęrne."'

XIII. 44–8.

Heofona ríce is gel·íc geh·ýddum gold-horde on þám æcere. Þone beh·ýtt se mann þe hine fint, and for his blisse gǽþ, and sęlþ eall þæt hé áh, and geb·ygþ þone æcer.

Ęft is heofona ríce gel·íc þám mangere þe sóhte þæt góde męre-grot. Þá hé funde þæt án déor-wierþe męregrot, þá éode hé, and sealde eall þæt hé áhte, and bohte þæt męre-grot.

Ęft is heofona ríce gel·íc ás·ęndum nętte on þá sǽ, and of ǽlcum fisc-cynne gadriendum. Þá híe þá þæt nętt upp át·ugon, and sǽton be þám strande, þá gec·uron híe þá gódan on hiera fatu, and þá yflan híe áw·urpon út.

XVIII. 12–14.

Gif hwelc mann hæfþ hund scéapa, and him losaþ án of þám, hú, ne forl·ǽtt hé þá nigon and hund-n·igontig on þám muntum, and gǽþ, and sécþ þæt án þe forw·earþ? And gif hit gel·impþ þæt hé ·hit fint, sóþlice ic éow sęcge þæt hé swíþor geb·lissaþ for þám ánum þonne for þám nigon and hundn·igontigum þe ná ne losodon.

XX. 1–16.

Heofona ríce is gel·íc þám híredes ealdre, þe on ǽrnemergen út éode áh·ýrian wyrhtan on his wín-geard. Gew·ordenre gec·wid-rǽdenne þám wyrhtum, hé sealde ǽlcum ánne pęning wiþ his dæges weorce, and ás·ęnde híe on his wíngeard. And þá hé út éode ymbe undern-tíd, hé ges·eah óþre on strǽte ídle stándan. Þá cwæþ hé: 'Gá gé on mínne wíngeard, and ic sęlle éow þæt riht biþ.' And híe þá férdon. Ęft hé út éode ymbe þá siextan and nigoþan tíd, and dyde þám swá gel·íce. Þá ymbe þá ęndlyftan tíd hé út éode, and funde óþre standende, and þá sægde hé: 'Hwý stande gé hér ealne dæg ídle?' Þá cwǽdon híe: 'For þám þe ús nán mann ne hýrode.' Þá cwæþ hé: 'And gá gé on mínne wíngeard.'

Sóþlice þá hit wæs ǽfen gew·orden, þá sægde se wíngeardes hláford his ger·éfan: 'Clipa þá wyrhtan, and ág·ief him hiera méde; ong·inn fram þám ýte·mestan óþ þone fyrmestan.' Eornostlice þá þá gec·ómon þe ymbe þá ęndlyftan tíd cómon, þá onf·éngon híe ǽlc his pęning. And þá þe þǽr ǽrest cómon, wéndon þæt híe scolden máre onf·ón; þá onf·éngon híe syndrige pęningas. Þá ong·unnon híe murcnian ong·éan þone híredes ealdor, and þus cwǽdon: 'Þás ýtemestan worhton áne tíd, and þú dydest híe gel·íce ús, þe bǽron byrþenna on þisses dæges hǽtan.' Þá cwæþ hé and-swariende hiera ánum: 'Éalá þú fréond, ne dó ic þé nánne téonan; hú, ne cóme þú tó mé tó wyrcenne wiþ ánum pęninge? Nim þæt þín is, and gá; ic wile þissum ýtemestum sęllan eall swá micel swá þé. Oþþe ne mót ic dón þæt ic wile? Hwæþer þe þín éage mánfull is for þám þe ic gód éom? Swá béoþ þa fyrmestan ýtemeste, and þá ýtemestan fyrmeste; sóþlice manige sind gec·lipode, and féa gec·orene.'

XXII. 2–14.

Heofona ríce is gel·íc þám cyninge þe macode his suna giefta, and sęnde his þéowas, and clipode þá gel·aþodan tó þám gieftum. Þá noldon híe cuman. Þá sęnde hé ęft óþre þéowas, and sægde þám gel·aþodum: 'Nú ic geg·earwode míne feorme: míne fearras and míne fuglas sind ofs·lægene, and eall mín þing sind gearu; cumaþ tó þám gieftum.' Þá forg·íemdon híe þæt, and férdon, sum tó his túne, sum tó his mangunge. And þá óþre námon his þéowas, and mid téonan ges·węncton, and ofs·lógon. Þá se cyning þæt geh·íerde, þá wæs hé ierre, and sęnde his hęre tó, and ford·yde þá man-slagan, and hiera burg forb·ærnde.

Þá cwæþ hé tó his þéowum: 'Witodlice þás giefta sind gearwe, ac þá þe gel·aþode wǽron ne sind wierþe. Gáþ nú tó wega gelǽtum, and clipiaþ tó þissum gieftum swá hwelce swá gé gem·éten.' Þá éodon þá þéowas út on þá wegas, and geg·adrodon ealle þá þe híe gem·étton, góde and yfle; þá wǽron þá gieft-hús mid sittendum mannum gefyldu.

Þá éode se cyning inn, þæt hé wolde ges·éon þá þe þǽr

sǽton, and þá ges·eah hé þǽr ánne mann þe næs mid gieftlicum réafe gescrýdd. Þá cwæþ hé: 'Lá, fréond, húmeta éodest þú inn, and næfdest gieftlic réaf?' Þá swígode hé. And se cyning cwæþ tó his þegnum: 'Geb·indaþ his handa and his fét, and weorpaþ hine on þá ýterran þéostru; þǽr biþ wóp and tóþa grist-bítung.' Witodlice manige sind gel·aþode, and féa gec·orene.

XXV. 1–13.

Þonne biþ heofona ríce gel·íc þám tíen fǽmnum, þe þá léoht-fatu námon, and férdon ongéan þone brýd-guman and þá brýd. Hiera fíf wǽron dysige, and fíf gléawe. And þá fíf dysigan námon léohtfatu, and ne námon nánne ele mid him; þá gléawan námon ele on hiera fatum mid þám léohtfatum. Þá se brýdguma ielde, þá hnappodon híe ealle, and slépon. Witodlice tó middre nihte man hríemde, and cwæþ: 'Nú se brýdguma cymþ, faraþ him tóg·éanes.' Þá ár·ison ealle þá fǽmnan, and glęngdon hiera léohtfatu. Þá cwǽdon þá dysigan to þám wísum: Sęllaþ ús of éowrum ele, for þám úre léohtfatu sind ác·węnctu.' Þá and-swarodon þá gléawan, and cwǽdon: 'Nese; þý læs þe wé and gé næbben genóh: gáþ tó þám cíependum, and bycgaþ éow ele.' Witodlice, þá híe férdon, and woldon bycgan, þá cóm se brýdguma; and þá þe gearwe wǽron éodon inn mid him tó þám gieftum; and séo duru wæs bel·ocen. Þá æt níehstan cómon þá óþre fǽmnan, and cwǽdon: 'Dryhten, Dryhten, lǽt ús inn.' Þá and-swarode hé him, and cwæþ: 'Sóþ ic éow sęcge, ne cann ic éow.' Witodlice, waciaþ, for þám þe gé nyton ne þone dæg ne þá tíd.

XXV. 14–30.

Sum mann fę́rde on ęl-þéodignesse, and clipode his

þéowas, and bet·ǽhte him his ǽhta. And ánum hé sealde fíf pund, sumum twá, sumum án: ǽg-hwelcum be his ágnum mægne; and férde sóna.

Þá férde se þe þá fíf pund under-f·éng, and ges·tríende óþru fíf. And eal-swá se þe þá twá underf·éng, ges·tríende óþru twá. Witodlice se þe þæt án underf·éng, férde, and bed·ealf hit on eorþan, and beh·ýdde his hláfordes feoh.

Witodlice æfter miclum fierste cóm þára þéowa hláford, and dihte him ger·ád. Þá cóm se þe þá fíf pund underf·éng, and bróhte óþru fíf, and cwæþ: 'Hláford, fíf pund þú sealdest mé; nú ic ges·tríende óþru fíf.' Þá cwæþ his hláford tó him: 'Béo blíþe, þú góda þéow and get·réowa: for þám þe þú wǽre get·réowe ofer lytlu þing, ic ges·ętte þe ofer miclu; gá intó þínes hláfordes blisse.' Þá cóm se þe þá twá pund underf·éng, and cwæþ: 'Hláford, twá pund þú mé sealdest; nú ic hæbbe ges·tríened óþru twá.' Þá cwæþ his hláford tó him: 'Geb·lissa, þú góda þéow and getréowa: for þám þe þú wǽre get·réowe ofer féa, ofer fela ic þé ges·ętte; gá on þínes hláfordes gef·éan.' Þá cóm se þe þæt án pund underf·éng, and cwæþ: 'Hláford, ic wát þæt þú eart heard mann: þú rípst þǽr þú ne séowe, and gaderast þǽr þú ne spręngdest. And ic férde ofd·rǽdd, and beh·ýdde þín pund on eorþan; hér þú hæfst þæt þín is.' Þá andswarode his hláford him, and cwæþ: 'þú yfla þéow and sláwa, þú wistest þæt ic rípe þǽr ic ne séowe, and ic gadrige þǽr ic ne strédde: hit geb·yrede þæt þú bef·æste mín feoh myneterum, and ic náme, þonne ic cóme, þæt mín is, mid þám gafole. Án·imaþ þæt pund æt him, and sęllaþ þám þe mé þá tíen pund bróhte. Witodlice ǽlcum þára þe hæfþ man sęlþ, and hé hæfþ gen·óh; þám þe næfþ, þæt him þyncþ þæt hé hæbbe, þæt him b·iþ ætb·rogden. And weorpaþ þone un-nyttan þéow on þá ýterran þéostru; þǽr biþ wóp and tóþa grist-bítung.'

III.

OLD TESTAMENT PIECES.

I.

Æfter þám sóþlice ealle męnn sprǽcon áne sprǽce. Þá þá híe férdon fram éast-dǽle, híe fundon ánne feld on Sennaar lande, and wunodon þǽro·n.

Þá cwǽdon híe him bet·wéonan: 'Uton wyrcan ús tigelan, and ǽlan híe on fýre!' Witodlice híe hæfdon tigelan for stán and tierwan for weal-lím. And híe cwǽdon: 'Uton timbrian ús ceastre, and stíepel óþ heofon héanne! uton weorþian úrne naman, ǽr þám þe wé síen tód·ǽlde geond ealle eorþan!'

Witodlice Dryhten ás·tág niþer, tó þám þæt hé ges·áwe þá burg and þone stíepel, þe Adames bearn get·imbrodon. And hé cwæþ: 'þis is án folc, and ealle híe sprecaþ án læden, and híe beg·unnon þis tó wyrcenne: ne ges·wícaþ híe ær þám þe hit gearu síe; sóþlice uton cuman and tód·ǽlan heora sprǽce!'

Swá Dryhten híe tód·ǽlde of þǽre stówe geond ealle eorþan. And for þám man nęmnde þá stówe *Babel* for þám þe þǽr wǽron tód·ǽlde ealle sprǽca.

II.

God wolde þá fandian Abrahames geh·íersumnesse, and clipode his naman, and cwæþ him þus tó: 'Nim þínne án-cęnnedan sunu Isaac, þe þú lufast, and far tó þám lande Visionis hraþe, and geo·ffra hine þǽr uppan ánre dúne.'

Abraham þá ár·ás on þǽre ilcan nihte, and férde mid twám cnapum tó þám fierlenum lande, and Isaac samod, on assum rídende.

Þá on þám þriddan dæge, þá híe þá dúne ges·áwon, þǽr þǽr híe tó scoldon tó ofs·léanne Isaac, þá cwæþ Abraham tó þám twám cnapum þus: 'Andbídiaþ éow hér mid þám assum sume hwíle! ic and þæt cild gáþ unc tó geb·iddenne, and wit siþþan cumaþ sóna ęft tó éow.'

Abraham þá hét Isaac beran þone wudu tó þǽre stówe and hé self bær his sweord and fýr. Isaac þá áscode Abraham his fæder: 'Fæder mín, ic áscige hwǽr séo offrung síe; hér is wudu and fýr.' Him andwyrde se fæder: 'God fore-scéawaþ, mín sunu, him self þá offrunge.'

Híe cómon þá tó þǽre stówe þe him ges·weotolode God; and hé þǽr weofod ár·ǽrde on þá ealdan wísan, and þone wudu gel·ógode swá swá hé hit wolde habban tó his suna bærnette, siþþan hé ofs·lægen wurde. Hé geb·and þá his sunu, and his sweord át·éah, þæt hé hine geo·ffrode on þá ealdan wísan.

Mid þám þe hé wolde þæt weorc beg·innan, þá clipode Godes ęngel arodlice of heofonum: 'Abraham!' Hé andwyrde sóna. Se ęngel him cwæþ tó: 'Ne ác·węle þú þæt cild, ne þíne hand ne ás·tręce ofer his sweoran! Nú ic onc·néow sóþlice þæt þú ond·rǽtst swíþe God, nú þú þínne án-cęnnedan sunu woldest ofs·léan for him.'

Þá bes·eah Abraham sóna under bæc, and ges·eah þǽr ánne ramm bet·wix þám brémlum be þám hornum geh·æftne, and hé hæfde þone ramm tó þǽre offrunge, and hine þǽr ofs·náþ Gode tó láce for his sunu Isaac. Hé hét þá stówe *Dominus videt*, þæt is 'God ges·ihþ,' and giet is ges·ægd swá, *In monte Dominus videbit*, þæt is, 'God ges·ihþ on dúne.'

Ęft clipode se ęngel Abraham, and cwæþ: 'Ic sægde þurh mé selfne, sægde se Ælm·ihtiga, nú þú noldest árian þínum áncęnnedum suna, ac þé wæs mín ęge máre þonne his líf, ic þé nú blétsige, and þínne of-spring gem·anig-fielde swá swá steorran on heofonum, and swá swá sand-ceosol on sǽ; þín ofspring sceal ágan hiera féonda geatu. And on þínum sǽde béoþ ealle þéoda geb·létsode, for þám þe þú geh·íersumodest mínre hǽse þus.'

Abraham þá gec·ierde sóna tó his cnapum, and férdon him hám sóna mid heofonlicre blétsunge.

III.

Sum cwén wæs on súþ-dǽle, Saba geh·áten, snotor and wís. Þá geh·íerde héo Salomones hlísan, and cóm fram þám súþernum gem·ǽrum to Salomone binnan Hierusalem mid micelre fare, and hiere olfendas bǽron súþerne wyrta, and déor-wierþe giem-stánas, and un-gerím gold. Séo cwén þá hæfde sprǽce wiþ Salomon, and sægde him swá hwæt swá héo on hiere heortan geþ·óhte. Salomon þá híe lǽrde, and hiere sægde ealra þára worda andgiet þe héo hine áscode. Þá ges·eah séo cwén Salomones wísdom, and þæt mǽre tempel þe hé get·imbrod hæfde, and þá lác þe man Gode offrode, and þæs cyninges manig-fealde þegnunga, and wæs tó þám swíþe ofw·undrod þæt héo næfde furþor nánne gást, for þám þe héo ne mihte ná furþor sméan. Héo cwæþ þá tó þám cyninge: 'Sóþ is þæt word þe ic geh·íerde on mínum earde be þé and be þínum wísdóme, ac ic nolde gel·íefan ǽr þám þe ic self hit ges·áwe. Nú hæbbe ic áf·andod þæt mé næs be healfum dǽle þín mǽrþo gec·ȳþed. Máre is þín wísdóm and þín weorc þonne se hlísa wǽre þe ic geh·íerde. Éadige sind þíne þegnas and þíne þéowas, þe simle ætf·oran þé standaþ, and þínne wísdom geh·íeraþ. Geb·létsod síe se ælm·ihtiga God, þe þé gec·éas and ges·ętte ofer Israhela ríce, þæt þú dómas sęte and riht-wísnesse.' Héo forg·eaf þám cyninge þá hund-twęlftig punda goldes, and ungerím déorwierþra wyrta and déorwierþra giemstána. Salomon éac forg·eaf þǽre cwéne swá hwæs swá héo gierndе æt him; and héo gew·ęnde ong·éan tó hiere éþle mid hiere þegnum. Salomon þá wæs gem·ǽrsod ofer eallum eorþlicum cyningum, and ealle þéoda gew·ilnodon þæt híe hine ges·áwen, and his wísdóm geh·íerden, and híe him manigfeald lác bróhton.

Séo cwén hæfde get·ácnunge þǽre hálgan gel·aþunge ealles cristenes folces, þe cóm tó þám ges·ibbsuman Criste tó geh·íerenne his wísdóm and þá god-spellican láre þe hé ás·tealde, and be onl·íehtunge þæs sóþan gel·éafan, and be þám tóweardan dóme, be úrre sáwle un-déadlicnesse, and be hyhte and wuldre þæs gem·ǽnelican ǽristes.

Séo cwén cóm tó Salomone mid miclum lácum on golde and on déorwierþum giemstánum and wyrt-brǽþum; and þæt bǽron olfendas. Séo gel·éaffulle gel·aþung, þe cymþ of ǽlcum earde tó Criste, bringþ him þás fore-sægdan lác æfter gástlicum and-giete. Héo offraþ him gold þurh sóþne gel·éafan, and wyrtbrǽþas þurh geb·edu, and déorwierþe giemmas þurh fægernesse gódra þéawa and háligra mægna. Be þissere gel·aþunge cwæþ se wítega tó Gode: 'Adstitit regina a dextris tuis, in vestitu deaurato, circumdata varietate,' þæt is, 'séo cwén stęnt æt þínre swíþran, on ofergyldum gierlan, ymbs·crýdd mid manigfealdre fágnesse.' Séo gástlice cwén, Godes gel·aþung, is geg·lęnged mid déorwierþre frætwunge and manigfealdum bléo gódra drohtnunga and mihta.

Héo sægde Salomone ealle hiere díegolnessa, and séo gel·aþung geo·penaþ Criste hiere inn-gehygd and þa díeglan geþ·óhtas on sóþre andetnesse.

Olfendas bǽron þá déorwierþan lác mid þǽre cwéne

intó Hierusalem; for þám þe þá hǽþnan, þe ǽr wǽron geh·oferode þurh gítsunge and atollice þurh leahtras, bǽron, þurh hiera gec·ierrednesse and gel·éafan, þá gástlican lác tó Cristes handum.

Séo cwén wundrode Salomones wísdómes, and his get·imbrunga, and þegnunga; and séo gel·aþung wundraþ Cristes wísdómes, for þám þe hé is sóþ wísdóm, and eall wísdóm is of him. Hé get·imbrode þá héalican heofonas and ealne middangeard, and ealle ges·ceafta ges·ętte on þrim þingum, *in mensura, et pondere, et numero*, þæt is, on gem·ete, ǫnd on hęfe, and on get·ele. Cristes þegnung is úre hǽlo and folca ál·íesednes, and þá sind ges·ǽlige þe him þegniaþ tó gec·wémednesse on þám gástlicum ger·ýnum.

Séo cwén sægde þæt hiere nǽre be healfum dǽle ges·ægd be Salomones mǽrþo, and séo gástlice cwén, Godes gel·aþung, oþþe geh·welc hálig sáwol, þonne héo cymþ tó þǽre heofonlican Hierusalem, þonne ges·ihþ héo micle máran mǽrþo and wuldor þonne hiere ǽr on lífe þurh wítegan oþþe apostolas gec·ýdd wǽre. Ne mæg nán éage on þissum lífe ges·éon, ne nán éare geh·íeran, ne nánes mannes heorte ás·méan þá þing þe God gearcaþ þám þe hine lufiaþ. Þá þing wé magon beg·ietan, ac wé ne magon híe ás·méan, ne ús nǽfre ne áþ·ríett þára góda gen·yht-sumnes.

Crist is ealra cyninga cyning, and swá swá ealle þéoda woldon ges·éon þone ges·ibbsuman Solomon, and his wísdóm geh·íeran, and him mislicu lác bróhton, swá éac nú of eallum þéodum gew·ilniaþ męnn tó ges·éonne þone ges·ibbsuman Crist þurh gel·éafan, and þone godspellican wísdóm geh·íeran, and híe him dæg-hwám-lice þá gástlican lác geo·ffriaþ on manigfealdum gem·etum.

IV.

On Cyres dagum cyninges wrégdon þá Babiloniscan þone

wítegan Daniel, for þám þe hé tów·earp hiera déofol-gield, and cwǽdon án-mód-lice tó þám fore-sægdan cyninge Cyrum: 'Betǽc ús Daniel, þe úrne god Bel tów·earp, and þone dracan ác·wealde þe wé on bel·íefdon; gif þú hine fors·tęntst, wé ford·ilgiaþ þé and þínne híred.'

Þá ges·eah se cyning þæt híe án-móde wǽron, and níe-dunga þone wítegan him tó handum ás·céaf. Híe þá hine áw·urpon intó ánum séaþe, on þám wǽron seofon léon, þám man sealde dæghwámlice twá hriþeru and twá scéap, ac him wæs þá oft·ogen ǽlces fódan siex dagas, þæt híe þone Godes mann áb·ítan scolden.

On þǽre tíde wæs sum óþer wítega on Judea lande, his nama wæs Abacuc, se bær his rifterum męte tó æcere. Þá cóm him tó Godes ęngel, and cwæþ: 'Abacuc, ber þone męte tó Babilone, and sęle Daniele, se þe sitt on þára léona séaþe.' Abacuc andwyrde þám ęngle: 'Lá léof, ne ges·eah ic nǽfre þá burg, ne ic þone séaþ nát.'

Þá se ęngel gel·ǽhte hine be þám feaxe, and hine bær tó Babilone, and hine sętte bufan þám séaþe. Þá clipode se Abacuc: 'þú Godes þéow, Daniel, nim þás lác þe þé God sęnde!' Daniel cwæþ: 'Mín Dryhten Hǽlend, síe þé lof and weorþ-mynd þæt þú mé gem·undest.' And hé þá þǽre sande bréac. Witodlice Godes ęngel þǽr-rihte mid swif-tum flyhte geb·róhte þone disc-þegn, Abacuc, þǽr hé hine ǽr gen·am.

Se cyning þá Cyrus on þám seofoþan dæge éode dréorig tó þára léona séaþe, and inn bes·eah, and efne þá Daniel sittende wæs ges·undfull onm·iddan þám léonum. Þá clipode se cyning mid micelre stefne: 'Mǽre is se God þe Daniel on bel·íefþ.' And hé þá mid þám worde hine át·éah of þám scræfe, and hét inn weorpan þá þe hine ǽr ford·ón woldon. Þæs cyninges hǽs wearþ hrædlice gef·ręmmed, and þæs wítegan éhteras wurdon ás·cofene bet·wix þá léon, and híe þǽrrihte mid grǽdigum ceaflum híe ealle tót·ǽron. Þá cwæþ se cyning: 'Forhtien and ond·rǽden ealle eorþ-búend Danieles God, for þám þe hé is Ál·íesend and Hǽlend, wyrcende tácnu and wundru on heofonan and on eorþan.'

VI.

Nabochodonosor, se hǽþena cyning, geh·ęrgode on Godes folce, on Judea lande, and for hiera mán-dǽdum God þæt geþ·afode. Þá gen·am hé þá máþm-fatu, gyldenu and silfrenu, binnan Godes temple, and tó his lande mid him gel·ǽdde. Hit gel·amp ęft siþþan þæt hé on swefne áne ges·ihþe be him selfum ges·eah, swá swá him siþþan áé·ode.

Æfter þissum ymb twelf mónaþ, éode se cyning binnan his healle mid or-mǽtre upp-áhafennesse, hęriende his weorc and his miht, and cwæþ: 'Hú, ne is þis séo micle Babilón, þe ic self get·imbrode tó cyne-stóle and tó þrymme, mé selfum to wlite and wuldre, mid mínum ágnum mægne and stręngþo?' Ac him clipode þǽrrihte tó swíþe ęgeslic stefn of heofonum, þus cweþende: 'Þú Nabochodonosor, þín ríce gew·ítt fram þé, and þú bist fram mannum áw·orpen, and þín wunung biþ mid wildéorum, and þú itst gærs, swá swá oxa, seofon géar, óþ þæt þú wite þæt se héalica God gew·ielt manna ríca, and þæt hé forg·iefþ ríce þám þe hé wile.'

Witodlice on þǽre ilcan tíde wæs þéos sprǽc gef·ylled ofer Nabochodonosor, and hé arn tó wuda, and wunode mid wildéorum, leofode be gærse, swá swá níeten, óþ þæt his feax wéox swá swá wíf-manna, and his næglas swá swá earnes clawa.

Ęft siþþan him forg·eaf se ælm·ihtiga Węaldend his gew·itt, and hé cwæþ: 'Ic Nabochodonosor áh·óf mín éagan upp tó heofonum, and mín andgiet mé wearþ forg·iefen, and ic þá blétsode þone híehstan God, and ic hęrede and wuldrode þone þe leofaþ on écnesse, for þám þe his miht is éce, and his ríce stęnt on mǽgþe and on mǽgþe. Ealle eorþ-búend sind tó náhte get·ealde on his wiþm·etennesse. Æfter his willan hé déþ ægþer ge on heofone ge on eorþan, and nis nán þing þe his mihte wiþst·ande, oþþe him tó cweþe 'hwý dést þú swá?' On þǽre tíde mín andgiet gew·ęnde tó mé, and ic bec·óm tó weorþ-mynde mínes cyne-ríces, and mín męnnisce hiw mé be·cóm. Míne witan mé sóhton, and mín mǽrþo wearþ geé·acnod. Nú eornostlice ic mǽrsige and wuldrige þone heofonlican cyning, for þám þe eall his weorc sind sóþ, and his wegas riht-wíse, and hé mæg geé·aþ-médan þá þe on módignesse faraþ.'

Þus geé·aþmédde se ælm·ihtiga God þone módigan cyning Nabochodonosor.

IV.

SAMSON.

Án mann wæs eardiende on Israhela þéode, Manue geh·áten, of þǽre mǽgþe Dan; his wíf wæs un-tíemend, and híe wunodon bútan cilde. Him cóm þá gangende tó Godes ęngel, and cwæþ þæt híe scolden habban sunu him gem·ǽnne; 'ne hé ealu ne drince nǽfre oþþe wín, ne náht fúles ne þicge; se biþ Gode hálig fram his cildháde; and man ne mót hine ęfsian oþþe bes·cieran, for þám þe hé ong·inþ tó ál·íesenne his folc, Israhela þéode, of Philistea þéowte.'

Héo ác·ęnde þá sunu, swá swá hiere sægde se ęngel, and hét hine Samson; and hé swíþe wéox; and God hine blétsode, and Godes gást wæs on him. Hé wearþ þá mihtig on micelre stręngþo, swá þæt hé gel·ǽhte áne léon be wege, þe hine áb·ítan wolde, and tób·rægd híe tó styccum, swelce he tót·ǽre sum éaþelic ticcen.

Hé beg·ann þá tó winnenne wiþ þá Philisteos, and hiera fela ofs·lóg and tó scame tucode, þéah þe híe onweald hæfden ofer his léode. Þá férdon þá Philistei forþ æfter Samsone, and héton his léode þæt híe hine ág·éafen tó hiera onwealde, þæt híe wrecan mihten hiera téon-rǽdenne mid tintregum on him. Híe þá hine geb·undon mid twám bæstenum rápum and hine gel·ǽddon tó þám folce. And þá Philisteiscan þæs fægnodon swíþe; urnon him tóg·éanes ealle hlýdende; woldon hine tintregian for hiera téonrǽdenne. Þá tób·rægd Samson begen his earmas, þæt þá rápas tó-burston þe hé mid geb·unden wæs. And hé gel·ǽhte þá sóna sumes assan cinn-bán þe hé þǽr funde, and gef·eaht wiþ híe, and ofs·lóg án þúsend mid þæs assan cinnbáne. Hé wearþ þá swíþe ofþ·yrst for þám wundorlican slęge, and bæd þone heofonlican God þæt hé him ás·ęnde drincan, for þám þe on þǽre néawiste næs nán wæterscipe. Þá arn of þám cinnbáne of ánum téþ wæter; and Samson þá dranc, and his Dryhtne þancode.

Æfter þissum hé férde tó Philistea lande, intó ánre byrig on hiera onwealde, Gaza geh·áten. And híe þæs fægnodon; bes·ętton þá þæt hús þe hé inne wunode; woldon hine gen·iman mid þám þe hé út éode on ǽrne-mergen, and hine ofs·léan. Hwæt þá Samson hiera sierwunga underg·eat; and ár·ás on middre nihte tóm·iddes his féondum, and gen·am þá burg-geatu, and geb·ær on his hrycge mid þám postum, swá swá híe bel·ocenu wǽron, upp tó ánre dúne tó ufeweardum þám cnolle; and éode swá or-sorg of hiera ges·ihþum.

Hine bes·wác swáþ·éah siþþan án wíf, Dalila geh·áten, of þám hǽþnan folce, swá þæt hé hiere sægde, þurh hiere swicdóm bep·ǽht, on hwám his stręngþo wæs and his wundorlic miht. Þá hǽþnan Philistei beh·éton hiere sceattas wiþ þám þe héo bes·wice Samson þone strangan. Þá áscode héo hine georne mid hiere ólǽcunge on hwám his miht wǽre; and he hiere andwyrde: 'Gif ic béo geb·unden mid seofon rápum, of sinum geworhte, sóna ic béo gew·ield.' Þæt swicole wíf þa beg·eat þá seofon rápas, and hé þurh sierwunge swá wearþ geb·unden. And him man cýþde þæt þǽr cómon his fíend; þá tób·ræc hé sóna þá rápas, swá swá hęfel-þrǽdas; and þæt wíf nyste on hwám his miht wæs. Hé wearþ ęft geb·unden mid eall-niwum rápum; and hé þá tób·ræc, swá swá þá óþre.

Héo bes·wác hine swáþ·éah, þæt hé hiere sægde æt níehstan: 'Ic éom Gode geh·álgod fram mínum cildháde; and ic næs nǽfre gegę·fsod, ne nǽfre bes·coren; and gif ic béo bes·coren, þonne béo ic un-mihtig, óþrum mannum gel·íc;' and héo lét þá swá.

Héo þá on sumum dæge, þá þá hé on slǽpe læg, forc·earf his seofon loccas, and áw·eahte hine siþþan; þá wæs hé swá unmihtig swá swá óþre męnn. And þá Philistei gef·éngon hine sóna, swá swá héo hine bel·ǽwde, and gel·ǽddon hine on-w·eg; and héo hæfde þone sceatt, swá swá him gew·earþ.

Híe þá hine áb·lęndon, and geb·undenne lǽddon on heardum racentéagum hám tó hiera byrig, and on cwearterne bel·ucon tó langre fierste: héton hine grindan æt hiera hand-cweorne. Þá wéoxon his loccas and his miht ęft on him. And þá Philistei full-b·líþe wǽron: þancodon hiera Gode, Dagon geh·áten, swelce híe þurh his fultum hiera féond gew·ielden.

Þá Philistei þá micle feorme gew·orhton, and ges·amnodon híe on sumre upp-flóra, ealle þá héafod-męnn, and éac swelce wíf-męnn, þréo þúsend manna on micelre blisse. And þá þá híe blíþost wǽron, þá bǽdon híe sume þæt Samson móste him macian sum gamen; and hine man sóna gef·ętte mid swíþlicre wáfunge, and héton hine standan bet·wix twám stǽnenum sweorum. On þám twám sweorum stód þæt hús eall gew·orht. And Samson þa plegode swíþe him ætf·oran; and gel·ǽhte þá sweoras mid swíþlicre mihte, and slóg híe tóg·ædre þæt híe sóna tób·urston; and þæt hús þá áf·éoll eall, þám folce tó déaþe, and Samson forþ mid, swá þæt hé micle má on his déaþe ác·wealde þonne hé ǽr cwic dyde.

V.

FROM THE CHRONICLE.

Breten íeg-land is eahta hund míla lang, and twá hund míla brád; and hér sind on þám íeglande fíf geþ·éodu: Ęnglisc, Brettisc, Scyttisc, Pihtisc, and Bóc-læden.

Ǽrest wǽron búend þisses landes Brettas. Þá cómon of Armenia, and ges·ǽton súþan-wearde Bretene ǽrest. Þá gel·amp hit þæt Peohtas cómon súþan of Scithian mid langum scipum, ná manigum; and þá cómon ǽrest on Norþ-ibernian upp; and þǽr bǽdon Scottas þæt híe þǽr mósten wunian. Ac híe noldon him líefan, for þon þe híe cwǽdon þæt híe ne mihten ealle ætg·ædre gew·unian þǽr. And þá cwǽdon þá Scottas: 'Wé magon éow hwæþre rǽd gel·ǽran; wé witon óþer íegland hér-beé·astan; þǽr gé magon eardian, gif gé willaþ; and gif hwá éow wiþst·ęnt, wé éow fultumiaþ þæt gé hit mægen gegán.'

Þá férdon þá Peohtas, and geférdon þis land norþan-weard; súþan-weard hit hæfdon Brettas, swá swá wé ǽr cwǽdon. And þá Peohtas him áb·ǽdon wíf æt Scottum on þá ger·ád þæt híe gec·uren hiera cyne-cynn á on þá wíf-healfe. Þæt híe héoldon swá lange siþþan.

And þá gel·amp ymbe géara ryne þæt Scotta sum dǽl gew·át of Ibernian on Bretene, and þæs landes sumne dǽl geé·odon; and wæs hiera hęre-toga Reoda geh·áten: fram þám híe sind gen·ęmnede Dalreodi.

Anno 449. Hér Martianus and Valentinus onf·éngon ríce, and rícsodon seofon winter.

And on hiera dagum, Hęngest and Horsa, fram Wyrtgeorne gel·aþode, Bretta cyninge, ges·óhton Bretene on þám stęde þe is gen·ęmned Ypwines-fléot, ǽrest Brettum tó fultume, ac híe ęft on híe fuhton.

Se cyning hét híe feohtan ong·éan Peohtas; and híe swá dydon, and sige hæfdon swá hwǽr swá híe cómon.

Híe þá sęndon tó Angle, and héton him sęndan máran fultum; and héton him sęcgan Bret-weala náhtnesse and þæs landes cysta. Híe þá sęndon him máran fultum. Þá cómon þá męnn of þrim mǽgþum Germanie: of Eald-seaxum, of Ęnglum, of Iotum.

Of Iotum cómon Cant-ware and Wiht-ware—þæt is séo mǽgþ þe nú eardaþ on Wiht—and þæt cynn on West-seaxum þe man nú-g·iet hǽtt 'Iotena cynn.' Of Eald-seaxum cómon Éast-seaxe, and Súþ-seaxe, and West-seaxe. Of Angle cómon—se á siþþan stód wéste bet·wix Iotum and Seaxum—Éast-ęngle, Middel-ęngle, Mierce, and ealle Norþhymbre.

455. Hér Hęngest and Horsa fuhton wiþ Wyrtgeorne þám cyninge in þǽre stówe þe is gec·weden Ægles-þrep; and his bróþor Horsan man ofs·lóg. And æfter þám Hęngest féng tó ríce, and Æsc his sunu.

457. Hér Hęngest and Æsc fuhton wiþ Brettas in þǽre stówe þe is gec·weden Cręcgan-ford, and þǽr ofs·lógon féower þúsend wera. And þá Brettas þá forl·éton Cęntland, and mid micle ęge flugon to Lunden-byrig.

473. Hér Hęngest and Æsc gef·uhton wiþ Wealas, and gen·ámon un-árímedlicu hęre-réaf, and þá Wealas flugon þá Ęngle swá swá fýr.

787. Hér nam Beorht-ríc cyning Offan dohtor Éad-burge. And on his dagum cómon ǽrest þréo scipu; and þá se

ger·éfa þǽr tó rád, and híe wolde drífan tó þæs cyninges túne, þý hé nyste hwæt híe wǽron; and hine man ofs·lóg. Þæt wǽron þá ǽrestan scipu Dęniscra manna þe Angelcynnes land ges·óhton.

851. Hér Ceorl ealdor-mann gef·eaht wiþ hǽþne męnn mid Defena-scíre æt Wicgan-beorge, and þǽr micel wæl ges·lógon, and sige námon.

And þý ilcan géare Æþel-stán cyning and Ealh-hęre dux micelne hęre ofs·lógon æt Sand-wíc on Cęnt; and nigon scipu gef·éngon, and þá óþru gef·líemdon; and hǽþne męnn ǽrest ofer winter sǽton.

And þý ilcan géare cóm féorþe healf hund scipa on Tęmese-múþan, and brǽcon Cant-wara-burg, and Lunden-burg, and gef·líemdon Beorht-wulf Miercna cyning mid his fierde; and férdon þá súþ ofer Tęmese on Súþrige; and him gef·eaht wiþ Æþel-wulf cyning and Æþel-beald his sunu æt Ác-léa mid West-seaxna fierde, and þǽr þæt mǽste wæl ges·lógon on hǽþnum hęre þe wé sęcgan híerdon óþ þisne andweardan dæg, and þǽr sige námon.

867. Hér fór se hęre of Éast-ęnglum ofer Humbre-múþan tó Eoforwíc-ceastre on Norþ-hymbre. And þǽr wæs micel un-geþwǽrnes þǽre þéode bet·wix him selfum, and híe hæfdon hiera cyning áw·orpenne Ós-bryht, and un-gecyndne cyning underf·éngon Ællan. And híe late on géare tó þám gec·ierdon þæt híe wiþ þone hęre winnende wǽron; and híe þéah micelne fierd geg·adrodon, and þone hęre sóhton æt Eoforwícceastre; and on þá ceastre brǽcon, and híe sume inne wurdon; and þǽr wæs un-gemetlic wæl ges·lægen Norþan-hymbra, sume binnan, sume bútan, and þá cyningas begen ofslægene; and séo láf wiþ þone hęre friþ nam.

VI.

KING EDMUND.

Sum swíþe gel·ǽred munuc cóm súþan ofer sǽ fram sancte Benedictes stówe, on Æþelrédes cyninges dæge, to Dúnstáne ærce-biscope, þrim géarum ǽr þám þe hé forþf·érde, and se munuc hátte Abbo. Þá wurdon híe æt sprǽce, óþ þæt Dúnstán reahte be sancte Éadmunde, swá swá Éadmundes sweord-bora hit reahte Æþelstáne cyninge, þá þá Dúnstán géong mann wæs, and se sweord-bora wæs fore·aldod mann. Þá ges·ętte se munuc ealle þá ger·ęccednesse on ánre béc, and ęft, þá þá séo bóc cóm tó ús, binnan féam géarum, þá áw·ęndon wé hit on Ęnglisc, swá swá hit héræ·fter stęnt. Se munuc þá Abbo binnan twám géarum gew·ęnde hám tó his mynstre, and wearþ sóna tó abbode ges·ętt on þám ilcan mynstre.

Eádmund se éadiga, Éast-ęngla cyning, wæs snotor and weorðfull, and weorþode simle mid æþelum þéawum þone ælm·ihtigan God. Hé wæs éaþ-mód and geþ·ungen, and swá án-rǽd þurhw·unode þæt hé nolde áb·úgan tó bismerfullum leahtrum, ne on náwþre healfe hé ne áh·ielde his þéawas, ac wæs simle gem·yndig þǽre sóþan láre: 'Gif þú eart tó héafod-męnn ges·ętt, ne áh·efe þú þé, ac béo bet·wix mannum swá swá án mann of him.' Hé wæs cystig wædlum and widewum swá swá fæder, and mid wel-willendnesse gew·issode his folc simle tó riht-wísnesse, and þám réþum stíerde, and ges·ǽliglice leofode on sóþum gel·éafan.

Hit gel·amp þá æt níehstan þæt þá Dęniscan léode férdon mid scip-hęre, hęrgiende and sléande wíde geond land, swá swá hiera gew·una is. On þám flotan wǽron þá fyrmestan héafod-męnn, Hinguar and Hubba, geá·nlǽhte þurh déofol, and híe on Norþhymbra-lande gel·ęndon mid æscum, and áw·éston þæt land, and þá léode ofs·lógon. Þá gew·ęnde Hinguar éast mid his scipum, and Hubba bel·áf on Norþhymbra-lande, gew·unnenum sige mid wæl-hréownesse Hinguar þá bec·óm tó Éast-ęnglum rówende on þám géare þe Ælfréd æþeling án and twentig géara wæs, se þe West-seaxna cyning siþþan wearþ mǽrę. And se fore-sægda Hinguar fǽrlice, swá swá wulf, on lande bes·tealcodę, and þá léode slóg, weras and wíf, and þá ungewittigan cildru, and to bismere tucode þá bilewitan Cristenan. Hé sęnde þá siþþan sóna tó þám cyninge béotlic ǽrende, þæt hé áb·úgan scolde tó his mann-rǽdenne, gif hé his feores róhte. Se ǽrend-raca cóm þá to Éadmunde cyninge, and Hinguares ǽrende him arodlice ábéad: 'Hinguar úre cyning, céne and sigefæst on sǽ and on lande, hæfþ fela þéoda gew·eald, and cóm nú mid fierde fǽrlice hér tó lande, þæt hé hér winter-setl mid his werode hæbbe. Nú hǽtt hé þé dǽlan þíne díeglan gold-hordas and þínra ieldrena ges·tréon arodlice wiþ hine, and þú béo his under-cyning, gif þú cwic béon wilt, for þám þe þú næfst þá miht þæt þú mæge him wiþs·tandan.'

Hwæt þá Éadmund cyning clipode ánne biscop þe him þá geh·ęndost wæs, and wiþ hine sméade hú hé þám réþan Hinguare andwyrdan scolde. Þá forhtode se biscop for þám fǽrlican gel·impe, and for þæs cyninges lífe, and cwæþ þæt him rǽd þúhte þæt hé tó þám geb·uge þe him béad Hinguar. Þá swígode se cyning, and bes·eah tó þǽre eorþan, and cwæþ þá æt níehstan cynelice him tó: 'Éalá þú biscop, to bismere sind get·awode þás earman land-léode, and mé nú léofre wǽre þæt ic on gef·eohte féolle wiþ þám þe mín folc móste hiera eardes brúcan.' And se biscop cwæþ: 'Éalá þú léofa cyning, þín folc líþ ofs·lægen, and þú næfst þone fultum þæt þú feohtan mæge, and þás flot-męnn cumaþ, and þé cwicne geb·indaþ, bútan þú mid fléame þínum feore geb·eorge, oþþe þú þé swá geb·eorge þæt þú búge tó him.' Þá cwæþ Éadmund cyning, swá swá hé full-c·éne wæs: 'þæs ic gew·ilnige and gew·ýsce mid móde þæt ic ána ne bel·ífe æfter mínum léofum þegnum, þe on hiera będdum wurdon mid bearnum and wífum fǽrlice ofs·lægene fram þissum flot-mannum. Næs mé nǽfre gew·unelic þæt ic worhte fléames, ac ic wolde swíþor sweltan, gif ic þorfte, for mínum ágnum earde, and se ælm·ihtiga God wát þæt ic nyle áb·úgan fram his bíg-gęngum ǽfre, ne fram his sóðre lufe, swelte ic, libbe ic.'

Æfter þissum wordum hé gew·ęnde tó þám ǽrend-racan þe Hinguar him tó sęnde, and sægde him un-forht: 'Witodlice þú wǽre nú wierþe slęges, ac ic nyle áf·ýlan on þínum fúlum blóde míne clǽnan handa, for þám þe ic Criste folgige, þé ús swá geb·ysnode; ac ic blíþelice wile béon ofs·lægen þurh éow, gif hit swá God fore-scéawaþ. Far nú swíþe hraþe, and sęge þínum réþan hláforde, 'ne áb·ýhþ nǽfre Éadmund Hinguare on lífe hǽþnum hęre-togan, bútan hé to Hǽlende Criste ǽrest mid gel·éafan on þissum lande geb·úge.'

Þá gew·ęnde se ǽrend-raca arodlice on-w·eg, and gem·étte be wege þone wæl-hréowan Hinguar mid ealre his fierde fúse tó Éadmunde, and sægde þám árleasan hú him gea·ndwyrd wæs. Hinguar bebéad þá mid bieldo þám scip-hęre þæt híe þæs cyninges ánes ealle cépan scolden, þe his hǽse fors·eah, and hine sóna bindan.

Hwæt þá Éadmund cyning, mid þám þe Hinguar cóm, stód innan his healle, þæs Hǽlendes gem·yndig, and áw·earp his wǽpnu; wolde gee·fen-lǽcan Cristes geb·ysnungum, þe forb·éad Petre mid wǽpnum tó winnenne wiþ þá wælhréowan Iudeiscan. Hwæt þá árléasan þá Éadmund geb·undon, and geb·ismrodon huxlice, and béoton mid saglum, and swá siþþan lǽddon þone gel·éaf-fullan cyning tó ánum eorð-fæstum tréowe, and tíegdon hine þǽr-tó mid heardum bęndum, and hine ęft swungon langlice mid swipum; and hé simle clipode bet·wix þám swinglum mid sóþum gel·éafan tó Hǽlende Criste; and þá hǽþnan þá for his gel·éafan wurdon wódlice ierre, for þám þe hé clipode Crist him tó fultume: híe scuton þá mid gafelocum him tó, swelce him to gamene, óþ þæt hé eall wæs bes·ętt mid hiera scotungum, swelce fles byrsta, swá swá Sebastianus wæs. Þá ges·eah Hinguar, se árléasa flotmann, þæt se æþela cyning nolde Criste wiþs·acan, ac mid ánrǽdum gel·éafan hine ǽfre clipode: hét hine þá beh·éafdian, and þá hǽþnan swá dydon. Bet·wix þám þe hé clipode to Criste þá-g·iet, þá tugon þá hǽþnan þone hálgan tó slęge, and mid ánum swęnge slógon him of þæt héafod, and his sáwol síþode ges·ǽlig tó Criste. Þǽr wæs sum mann geh·ęnde geh·ealden, þurh God beh·ýdd þám hǽþnum, þe þis geh·íerde eall, and hit ęft sægde, swá swá wé hit sęcgaþ hér.

Hwæt þá se flot-hęre férde ęft tó scipe, and beh·ýddon þæt héafod þæs hálgan Éadmundes on þám þiccum brémlum, þæt hit beb·yrged ne wurde. Þá æfter fierste siþþan híe áf·arene wǽron, cóm þæt land-folc tó, þe þǽr tó láfe wæs, þǽr hiera hláfordes líc læg bútan héafde, and wurdon swíþe sárige for his slęge on móde, and húru þæt híe næfden þæt héafod tó þám bodige. Þá sægde se scéawere þe hit ǽr ges·eah, þæt þá flotmęnn hæfden þæt héafod mid him; and wæs him geþ·úht, swá swá hit wæs full-s·óþ, þæt híe beh·ýdden þæt héafod on þám holte forh·wega.

Híe éodon þá ęndemes ealle tó þám wuda, sécende geh·wǽr, geond þýflas and brémlas, gif híe á-hwǽr mihten gem·étan þæt héafod. Wæs éac micel wundor þæt án wulf wearþ ás·ęnd, þurh Godes wissunge, to bew·ęrienne þæt héafod wiþ þá óþru déor ofer dæg and niht. Híe éodon þá sécende and simle clipiende, swá swá hit gew·unelic is þám þe on wuda gáþ oft: 'Hwǽr eart þú nú, gef·éra?' And him and-wyrde þæt héafod: 'Hér, hér, hér;' and swá gel·óme clipode andswariende him eallum, swá oft swá hiera ǽnig clipode, óþ þæt híe ealle bec·ómon þurh þá clipunge him tó. Þá læg se grǽga wulf þe bew·iste þæt héafod, and mid his twám fótum hæfde þæt héafod bec·lypped, grǽdig and hungrig, and for Gode ne dorste þæs héafdes onb·yrgan, ac héold hit wiþ déor. Þá wurdon híe of-w·undrode þæs wulfes hierd-rǽdenne, and þæt hálige héafod hám fęredon mid him, þanciende þám Ælm·ihtigan ealra his wundra. Ac se wulf folgode forþ mid þám héafde, óþ þæt híe tó túne cómon, swelce hé tam wære, and gew·ęnde ęft siþþan tó wuda ong·éan.

Þá land-léode þá siþþan lęgdon þæt héafod tó þám hálgan bodige, and beb·yrigdon swá híe sélost mihton on swelcre hrædunge, and cirican ár·ǽrdon sóna him onu·ppan. Ęft þá on fierste, æfter fela géarum, þá séo hęrgung ges·wác, and sibb wearþ forg·iefen þám ges·węnctan folce, þá féngon híe tóg·ædre, and worhton áne cirican weorþlice þám hálgan, for þám þe gel·óme wundru wurdon æt his byrgenne, æt þám geb·ed-húse þǽr hé beb·yrged wæs. Híe woldon þá fęrian mid folclicre weorþmynde þone hálgan líchaman, and lęcgan innan þǽre cirican. Þá wæs micel wundor þæt hé wæs eall swá geh·ál swelce hé cwic wǽre, mid clǽnum líchaman, and his sweora wæs geh·ǽled, þe ǽr wæs forsl·ægen, and wæs swelce án seolcen þrǽd ymbe his sweoran, mannum tó sweotolunge hú hé ofsl·ægen wæs. Éac swelce þá wunda þe þá wælhréowan hǽþnan mid gel·ómum scotungum on his líce macodon, wǽron geh·ǽlde þurh þone heofonlican God;

and hé líþ swá onsund óþ þisne and-weardan dæg, andbídiende ǽristes and þæs écan wuldres. His líchama ús cýþþ, þe líþ un-formolsnod, þæt hé bútan forl·igre hér on worulde leofode, and mid clǽnum lífe tó Criste síþode.

Sum widewe wunode, Óswyn geh·áten, æt þæs hálgan byrgenne, on geb·edum and fæstennum manigu géar siþþan. Séo wolde ęfsian ǽlce géare þone sanct, and his næglas ceorfan síeferlice mid lufe, and on scríne healdan tó hálig-dóme on weofode. Þá weorþode þæt land-folc mid gel·éafan þone sanct and Þéodréd biscop þearle mid giefum on golde and on seolfre, þám sancte tó weorþmynde.

Þá cómon on sumne sǽl un-gesǽlige þéofas eahta on ánre nihte tó þám ár-weorþan hálgan: woldon stelan þá máþmas þe męnn þider bróhton, and cunnodon mid cræfte hú híe inn cuman mihten. Sum slóg mid slęcge swíþe þá hæpsan, sum hiera mid féolan féolode ymbú·tan, sum éac underd·ealf þá duru mid spade, sum hiera mid hlǽddre wolde onl·úcan þæt éag-þyrel; ac híe swuncon on ídel, and earmlice férdon, swá þæt se hálga wer híe wundorlice geb·and, ǽlcne swá hé stód strútiendne mid tóle, þæt hiera nán ne mihte þæt morþ gef·ręmmam ne híe þanon ás·tyrian; ac stódon swá óþ mergen. Męnn þá þæs wundrodon, hú þá weargas hangodon, sum on hlǽddre, sum léat to ged·elfe, and ǽlc on his weorce wæs fæste geb·unden. Híe wurdon þá geb·róhte tó þám biscope ealle, and hé hét híe áh·ón on héam gealgum ealle; ac hé næs ná gem·yndig hú se mildheorta God clipode þurh his wítegan þás word þe hér standaþ: 'Eos qui ducuntur ad mortem eruere nę cesses,' 'þá þe man lǽtt tó déaþe ál·íes híe út simle.' And éac þá hálgan canónes béc geh·ádodum forb·éodaþ ge biscopum ge préostum tó béonne ymbe þéofas, for þám þe hit ne geb·yreþ þám þe béoþ gec·orene Gode to þegnienne þæt híe geþ·wǽrlǽcan scylen on ǽniges mannes déaþe, gif híe béoþ Dryhtnes þegnas. Ęft þá þéodréd biscop scéawode his béc, hé siþþan beh·réowsode mid géomrunge þæt hé swá réþne dóm sętte þám ungesǽligum þéofum, and hit bes·árgode ǽfre óþ his lífes ęnde, and þá léode bæd georne þæt híe him mid fæsten fullice þríe dagas, biddende þone Ælm·ihtigan þæt hé him árian scolde.

On þám lande wæs sum mann, Léofstán geh·áten, ríce for worulde, un-gewittig for Gode; se rád tó þám hálgan mid rícetere swíþe, and hét him ætí·ewan orgellice swíþe þone hálgan sanct, hwæþer hé ges·und wǽre; ac swá hraþe swá hé ges·eah þæs sanctes líchaman, þá áw·édde hé sóna, and wæl-hréowlice grymetode, and earmlice geę·ndode yflum déaþe. Þis is þám gel·íc þe se gel·éaffulla pápa Gregorius sægde on his gesętnesse be þám hálgan Laurentie, þe líþ on Róme-byrig, þæt męnn woldon scéawian hú hé lǽge ge góde ge yfle; ac God híe ges·tilde swá þæt þǽr swulton on þǽre scéawunge seofon męnn ætg·ædre; þá geswicon þá óþre tó scéawienne þone martyr mid męnniscum ged·wylde.

Fela wundra wé geh·íerdon on folclicre sprǽce be þám hálgan Éadmunde, þe wé hér nyllaþ on gew·rite sęttan, ac híe wát geh·wá. On þissum hálgan is sweotol, and on swelcum óþrum, þæt God ælm·ihtig mæg þone mann ár·ǽran ęft on dómes dæge onsundne of eorþan, se þe hielt Éadmund hálne his líchaman óþ þone miclan dæg, þéah þe hé on moldan cóme. Wierþe wǽre séo stów for þám weorþfullan hálgan þæt híe man weorþode and wel gel·ógode mid clǽnum Godes þéowum tó Cristes þéowdóme; for þám þe se hálga is mǽrra þonne męnn mægen ás·méan. Nis Angel-cynn bed·ǽled Dryhtnes hálgena, þonne on Ęngla-lande licgaþ swelce hálgan swelce þes hálga cyning, and Cúþberht se éadiga and sancte Æþelþrýþ on Elig, and éac hiere sweostor, onsund on líchaman, gel·éafan tó trymmunge. Sind éac fela óþre on

Angel-cynne hálgan, þe fela wundra wyrcaþ, swá swá hit wíde is cúþ, þám Ælm·ihtigan tó lofe, þe híe on gel·íefdon. Crist ges·wẹotolaþ mannum þurh his mǽre hálgan þæt hé is ælm·ihtig God þe wyrcþ swelc wundru, þéah þe þá earman Iudeiscan hine eallunga wiþs·ócen, for þám þe híe sind áw·iergde, swá swá híe wýscton him selfum. Ne béoþ nán wundru gew·orht æt hie·ra byrgennum, for þám þe híe ne gel·íefaþ on þone lifiendan Crist; ac Crist ges·weotolaþ mannum hwǽr se góda gẹl·éafa is, þonne hé swelc wundru wyrcþ þurh his hálgan wíde geond þás eorþan, þæs him síe wuldor and lof á mid his heofonlicum Fæder and þám Hálgan Gáste, á bútan ęnde.

NOTES.

The references marked 'Gr.' are to the pages and paragraphs of the grammar; paragraph-references in ( ) are to the numbered paragraphs in the grammar.

I. SENTENCES.

Line 2. **sé.** Gr. 21. 1.

þis sind. Gr. 45. 2.

l. 6. **sęlþ.** Gr. 45. 5.

l. 7. **séo ælmesse.** Gr. 44. 3.

l. 12. **geworhte.** Gr. 46. (3).

l. 16. **hiera.** Gr. 41. 3.

nǽfre . . ne . . nánes. Gr. 52. 2. *ne wæs* is usually contracted into *næs*; the full form is used here because the *wæs* is emphatic.

l. 17. **hét ofsléan.** Gr. 50. 4.

l. 23. **Æþelréd cyning.** Gr. 42. 6.

l. 24. **Æsces-dún,** *sf.* Ashdown, literally 'hill (or down) of the ash tree.'

l. 27. **wile** here denotes *repetition,* = 'is in the habit of.' Cp. l. 52.

l. 28. **þonne** is correlative with *gif* (l. 26), Gr. 52. 3.

l. 37. **ælmihtiga.** Gr. 43. (4).

l. 43. **éower se heofonlica Fæder.** This insertion of the definite article between a possessive pronoun and an adjective is frequent.

l. 50. **béo.** Gr. 48. (6).

l. 52. **tó,** for.

l. 56. **twęntig wintra.** Gr. 18.

l. 58. **Déofol.** Gr. 44. 1.

l. 60. **scortan.** Gr. 43. (2).

l. 61. **fisca.** Gr. 41. 3.

l. 63. **þám,** those.

hider on land, lit. hither to land, = to this land.

l. 74. **blétsian.** The older form of this word is *blédsian*. It is a derivative of *blód,* like *rícsian* from *ríce,* with mutation of the root vowel. Its original meaning was to 'sprinkle with blood,' and hence, in heathen times, to 'consecrate,' especially to consecrate an altar by sprinkling it with the blood of the victim.

l. 80. **godspell.** The original form of this word was probably *gód-spell*='good tidings,' a literal translation of the Greek *euaggélion.* Afterwards the first vowel was shortened before the following consonant-group, or else *god* was directly substituted for *gód,* as giving a more evident meaning, the result being that the word was taken in the sense of 'God's tidings.' In this form it was adopted into Icelandic (guðspiall) and Old High German (gotespel), having been introduced by the Old English missionaries.

biþ. Gr. 45. 5.

l. 82. **híe.** Gr. 20.

l. 89. **him on ǽlce healfe,** lit. 'to (for) themselves on each side,' = on every side (of themselves).

l. 92. **rihtne.** Gr. 42. 5.

l. 93. **Æþelwulf-ing.** Gr. 38.

l. 101. **fare gé.** Gr. 22. 7.

l. 106. **forsǽwon.** A plural verb after a singular noun of multitude is common in O. E. as in other languages.

l. 114. **cwǽde.** Gr. 48. (5).

l. 118. **mæge.** Compare Gr. 47. (B. 1).

l. 119. **síe.** Gr. 47 (A).

l. 120. **Scotland** is here used in its older sense of 'Ireland.' Compare the first extract from the Chronicle, p. 25 below.

l. 121. **his.** Gr. 41. 3.

l. 123. **healden.** Gr. 48. (4).

l. 124. **wǽre.** Gr. 47. (B. 1).

l. 132. **se þe.** Gr. 21. 4.

l. 135. **þæt.** Gr. 21. 4, 52. 3.

l. 137. **on éare.** Gr. 51. 2.

l. 138. **gewęndon him,** lit. 'they went for-themselves'; a reflexive pronoun in the dative, Gr. 40. (1), is often added to verbs of motion.

l. 139. **dó gé.** Gr. 22. 7.

l. 142. **gréte.** Compare Gr. 49. 8.

l. 145. **swelce,** adverb, 'as it were.'

l. 151. **nime.** Gr. 48. (6).

l. 166. **ofslægenne.** Gr. 46. 5.

l. 176. **geweorþen.** Gr. 47. (B. 1.)

l. 191. **béon.** Gr. 48. (2).

II. FROM THE GOSPEL OF ST. MATTHEW.

l. 1. **þás mín word.** Gr. 43. 8.

l. 16. **áweorpe.** Gr. 49. (8).

l. 20. **hit** refers back to *sǽd*, l. 18.

l. 22. **upp sprungenre sunnan.** Gr. 41. 2.

l. 28. **is geworden.** An over-literal rendering of the Latin *factum est.*

l. 32. **hine,** reflexive, Gr. 19.

l. 40. **tó forbærnenne.** We see here how out of the active 'in order to burn it' may be developed the passive 'in order that it may be burnt,' as in the modern E. 'a house to let.' Compare Gr. 50. 4. (1).

l. 52. **on hiera fatu.** Compare I. 137.

l. 60. **gewordenre geowidrǽdenne þám wyrhtum.** A very stiff adaptation of the ablative absolute of the original, 'conventione autem facta cum operariis.' *þám wyrhtum* is to be taken as a dative of the person affected (Gr. 41).

l. 67. **dyde þám swá gelíce.** The Latin has simply 'fecit similiter.' The sense is 'did like to it' (like his former proceeding), the *swá* being pleonastic.

l. 86. **þæt.** Gr. 21. 4.

l. 90. **suna,** dative, 'for his son.'

l. 106. **glefthús.** *hús* must here be taken in the sense of 'hall,' 'chamber.' In Icelandic the plural *hús* is regularly used to denote the group of buildings (often detached) constituting a house or homestead, he kitchen, for instance, which was originally detached, being still called *eldhús* (fire-house).

l. 107. **þæt hé wolde geséon.** This clause is due to a confusion of two constructions, (1) *hé wolde geséon,* (2) *þæt* (in order that) *hé ges·áwe.*

III. OLD TESTAMENT PIECES.

The first two pieces are taken from Ælfric's translation of the Heptateuch, first published by Thwaites in his Heptateuchus, and afterwards by Grein as vol. i. of his *Bibliothek der angelsächsischen Prosa*—Genesis xi. and xxii. The other three are from Ælfric's Homilies (edited by Thorpe)—ii. 584 foll., i. 570, ii. 432.

l. 4. **him betwéonan.** Gr. 51. 5.

l. 17. **for þám .. for þám þe,** correlative, the first demonstrative, the second relative.

l. 28. **tó scoldon.** This use of *sceal* with a verb of motion understood is very common.

l. 36. **him self.** *him* is the reflexive dative of interest referring to *God*—literally, 'God him-self will appoint for-himself.' In such constructions we see the origin of the modern *himself, themselves.*

ll. 46, 47. **nú .. nú,** correlative, = now .. now that, the second *nú* being almost causal (since).

l. 51. **hæfde .. tó,** took .. for.

l. 52. **Gode tó láce.** Gr. 40. (1).

l. 57. **mín ęge,** objective genitive, the fear of me.

máre, neut. 'a greater thing,' 'something more important.'

l. 81. **máre.** Gr. 40. 1.

l. 82. **wǽre.** Gr. 49. (7).

l. 89. **hwæs** is governed by *giernde,* by 'attraction.'

l. 135. **micle,** adverb.

l. 137. **wǽre.** Gr. 49. (7).

l. 174. **ǽr genam.** Gr. 46. 6.

l. 200. **fram mannum.** *fram* here, as usual, denotes the agent (with) in passive constructions.

l. 202. **wite.** Compare Gr. 48. (3) and 49. (8).

IV. SAMSON.

From Ælfric's translation of the Book of Judges in Thwaites' Heptateuch.

l. 8. **onginþ to álíesenne,** will release. *onginnan* is often used pleonastically in this way.

l. 35. **Gaza geháten.** When a name together with *geháten* is put in apposition to another noun it is left undeclined, contrary to the general principle (Gr. 42. 6).

l. 41. **swá swá híe belocenu wǽron,** locked as they were.

ufeweardum þám oncolle. Gr. 43. 2.

l. 46. **wæs,** consisted.

l. 51. **geworhte.** We should expect *geworhtum* (Gr. 42. 5). Perhaps the nom. is due to confusion with the construction with a relative clause—*þe of sinum geworhte sind.*

l. 74. **Dagon geháten.** Compare l. 35.

swelce, 'on the ground that'—'because (as they said).'

l. 81. **héton.** Compare I. 106.

l. 87. **forþ** is often used pleonastically in this way with *mid.*

V. FROM THE CHRONICLE.

l. 2. **hér sind**, there are here. *hér* is here used analogously to *þár*, as in II. 3 and the modern E. *there are*. Cp. also l. 12 below.

geþéodu, languages as the test of nationality. It is believed that Latin was still spoken as a living language by the Romanized Britons at the time of the venerable Bede (eighth century), from whose Church History this section was taken by the compilers of the Chronicle.

l. 5. **Armenia** is an error for *Armorica*.

l. 6. **Scithie**, Scythia.

l. 8. **Norþibernie**, North of Ireland.

l. 24. **hér**, at this date—at this place in the series of entries which constitute the Chronicle.

l. 26. **Wyrtgeorn** is the regular development of an earlier * *Wurtigern* from the British *Vortigern*.

l. 28. **Ypwinesflēot** has not been identified; some say Ebbsfleet.

l. 45. **Æglesþrep**, Aylesford.

l. 49. **Cręcganford**, Crayford.

l. 61. **hǽþne męnn**, Danes.

l. 62. **mid Defena-scíre**, literally 'together with Devonshire,' that is 'with a force of Devonshire men.'

l. 64. **dux** is here written instead of *ealdormann*. So also we find *rex* for *cyning*.

l. 65. **Sandwíc**, Sandwich.

l. 68. **féorþe healf hund**, fourth half = three and a half. This is the regular way of expressing fractional numbers, as in the German *viertehalb*.

l. 71. **Súþrige**, Surrey.

l. 73. **Ácléa**, Ockley.

l. 76. **se hęre**, the Danish army. *hęre* got a bad sense, through its association with *hęrgian* (to harry), and hence is applied only to a plundering, marauding body of men. In the Laws *hęre* is defined as a gang of thieves more than thirty-five in number. The national English army (militia) is called *fierd*, l. 71, 3 above.

Humbremúþa, mouth of the Humber.

l. 77. **Eoforwíc**, York; a corruption of *Eboracum*.

l. 84. **inne wurdon**, got in.

l. 85. **sume**. Compare IV. 51.

VI. KING EDMUND.

From Ælfric's Lives of the Saints, now in course of publication for the Early English Text Society by Prof. Skeat. The present life has been printed only by Thorpe in his *Analecta Anglosaxonica* from a very late MS. It is here given from the older MS., Cott. Jul. E. 7.

It will be observed that the present piece is in alliterative prose, that is, with the letter-rime of poetry, but without its metrical form. The alliteration is easily discernible:—cóm *s*úþan ofer *s*ǽ fram *s*ancte Benedictes *s*tówe; *d*æge, tó *D*únstáne, &c.

l. 1. **sancte** is an English modification of the Latin genitive *sancti.*

l. 5. **sancte** is here the E. dative inflection, *sanct* having been made into a substantive.

l. 70. **worhte fléames.** This construction of *wyrcan* with a genitive is frequent.

l. 76. **wǽre,** subj. Gr. 48. (6).

l. 85. **fúse.** The correct reading is probably *fúsne*, but the plural *fúse* may be taken to refer to Hinguar and his men collectively.

l. 176. **swá þæt** does not denote result here, but is explanatory—'namely by being bound ...'

l. 178. **híe,** reflexive.

ll. 179, 180. **þæs .. hú,** correlative.

l. 185. The reference is apparently to Proverbs xxiv. 11, which (in the Vulgate) runs thus: 'Erue eos qui ducuntur ad mortem.'

l. 200. **hwæþer,** (that he might see) whether ...

l. 215. **líchaman,** instrumental dative (Gr. 41) of defining.

GLOSSARY.

The order is strictly alphabetical (þ following *t*), except that words with the prefix *ge* are put in the order of the letter that follows the *ge* (*gebed* under *b*, &c.).

The following abbreviations are used :—

sm., *sn.*, *sf.* masc., neut., fem. substantive.
sv. strong verb.
wv. weak verb.
swv. strong-weak verb (preterito-present).

The others require no explanation.

The numbers after *sv.* refer to the classes of strong verbs in the grammar.

Numbers in ( ) refer to the pages of the grammar.

Words in [ ] are Latin (and Greek) originals or cognate Old E. words. The latter are only referred to when the connection can be proved by the phonetic laws given in the grammar.

Á, *av.* ever, always.
abbod, *sm.* abbot [*Latin* abbatem].
á-b·éodan, *sv.* 7, *w. dat.* (offer), announce.
á-b·iddan, *sv.* 5, ask for, demand.
á-b·ítan, *sv.* 6, devour.
á-b·lęndan, *wv.* blind [blind].
á-b·recan, *sv.* 4, break into, take (city).
á-b·úgan, *sv.* 7, bend; swerve, turn.
ac, *cj.* but.
á-c·ęnnan, *wv.* bring forth, bear (child).
á-c·węllan, *wv.* kill.
á-c·węncan, *wv.* extinguish.
á-d·rúgian, *wv.* dry up, *intr.* [drýge].
á-d·wǽscan, *wv.* extinguish.
æcer, *sm.* field.
æþele, *aj.* noble, excellent.
æþeling, *sm.* prince.
ǽfen, *sm.* evening.
ǽfre, *av.* ever, always.
æfter, *av.*, *prep. w. dat.* after—æfter þám, after that, afterwards; according to, by.
ǽg-hwelc, *prn.* each.
ǽgþer, *prn.* either, each—*cj.* ǽgþer ge . . ge, both . . and [=ǽg-hwæþer].
ǽht, *sf.* property [ágan].
ǽlan, *wv.* burn.
ǽlc, *aj.* each.
ælmesse, *sf.* alms, charity [*Greek* eleēmosúnē].
æl-m·ihtig, *aj.* almighty.
ǽnig, *aj.* any [án].
ǽr, *prep. w. dat.* before (of time) ǽr þám þe, *cj.* before.
ǽr, *av.* formerly, before; *superl.* ǽrest, *adj. and adv.*, first.
ærce-biscop, *sm.* archbishop [*Latin* archiepiscopus].
ǽrende, *sn.* errand, message.

ǽrend-raca, *sm.* messenger.
ǽ-rist, *sfm.* (rising again), resurrection [árisan].
ǽrne-mergen, *sm.* early morning.
æsc, *sm.* (ash-tree); war-ship.
æt, *prp. w. dat.* at; *deprivation*, from; *origin, source*—ábǽdon wíf æt him, 'asked for wives from them;' *specification, defining*—wurdon æt sprǽce, 'fell into conversation.'
æt-b·regdan, *sv.* 3 (snatch away), deprive of.
æt-f·oran, *prp. w. dat.* before.
æt-g·ædre, *av* together.
æt-íewan, *wv. w. dat.* show.
ǽton, *see* **etan**.
á-f·andian, *wv.* experience, find out [findan].
á-f·aran, *sv.* 2, go away, depart.
á-f·eallan, *sv.* 1, fall.
á-f·édan, *wv.* feed.
á-f·ýlan, *wv.* defile [fúl].
á-fyrht, *aj.* frightened [*past partic. of* áf·yrhtan *from* forht].
ágan, *swv.* possess.
á-g·án, *sv.* happen.
ágen, *aj.* own [*originally past partic. of* ágan].
á-g·iefan, *sv.* 5, *w. dat.* give, render.
áh, *see* **ágan**.
á-h ębban, *sv.* 2, raise, exalt.
á-h·ieldan, *wv.* incline.
á-h·ón, *sv.* 1, hang, *trans.*
á-h·réosan, *sv.* 7, fall.
áhte, *see* **ágan**.
á-hwǽr, *av.* anywhere.
á-h·ýrian, *wv.* hire.
á-l·íesan, *wv.* (loosen), release; redeem [léas].
á-l·íesed-nes, *sf.* redemption.
á-l·íesend, *sm.* redeemer.
án, *aj.* one (*always strong*); a certain one, certain; alone (*generally weak*); *gen. pl.* ánra *in* ánra gehwelc, 'each one.'
án-cęnned, *aj.* (*past partic.*) (only-born), only (child).
and, *cj.* and.
and-bídian, *wv. w. gen.* wait, expect [bídan].
andet-nes, *sf.* confession.
andettan, *wv.* confess.
and-giet, *sn.* sense, meaning; understanding, intelligence.
and-swarian, *wv. w. dat.* answer [andswaru].
and-swaru, *sf.* answer [swęrian].
and-weard, *aj.* present.
and-wyrdan, *wv. w. dat.* answer [word].
Angel, *sm.* Anglen (a district in Slesvig).
Angel-cynn, *sn.* English nation, England.
á-n·iman, *sv.* 4, take away.
án-lǽcan, *wv.* unite.
án-mód, *aj.* unanimous.
án-mód-lice, *av.* unanimously.
án-rǽd, *aj.* (of one counsel) constant, firm, resolute.
apostol, *sm.* apostle.
ár, *sf.* mercy; honour.
á-r·ǽran, *wv.* raise, build [árísan].
árian, *wv. w. dat.* honour; spare, have mercy on [ár].
á-r·ísan, *sv.* 6, arise.
ár-léas, *aj.* wicked.
arn, *see* **iernan**.
arod, *aj.* quick, bold.
arod-lice, *av.* quickly, readily, boldly.
ár-weorþ, *adj.* worthy of honour, venerable.
áscian, *wv.* ask.
á-sc·úfan, *sv.* 7, thrust.
á-s·ęndan, *wv.* send.
á-s·ęttan, *wv.* set, place.
á-s·méan, *wv.* consider, think of, conceive.
assa, *sm.* ass.
á-st·ęllan, *wv.* institute.
á-st·ígan, *sv.* 6, ascend, descend.
á-st·ręccan, *wv.* stretch out, extend.
á-st·yrian, *wv.* stir, move.
á-t·éon, *sv.* 7, draw out, draw, take.
atol-lic, *aj.* deformed.
á-þ·réotan, *sv.* 7, fail, run short.

á-w·ęccan, *wv.* awake, arouse [wacian].
á-w·édan, *wv.* go mad [wód].
á-w·ęndan, *wv.* turn; translate.
á-w·eorpan, *sv.* 3, throw, throw away; depose (king).
á-w·éstan, *wv.* lay waste, ravage.
á-w·ierged, *aj.* cursed, accursed [*past. partic. of* áwiergan, *from* wearg].
á-wiht, *prn.* aught, anything.
á-w·rítan, *sv.* 6, write.
á-w·yrtwalian, *wv.* root up.

B.

Bæc, *sn.* back—under bæc, behind.
bæd, *see* **biddan.**
bǽdon, *see* **biddan.**
bærnan, *wv.* burn, *trans.* [beornan].
bærnett, *sn.* burning.
bǽron, *see* **beran.**
bæst, *sm.* bast.
bæsten, *aj.* of bast.
be, *prep. w. dat.* by; about, concerning.
beald, *aj.* bold.
bearn, *sn.* child [beran].
béatan, *sv.* 1, beat.
be-b·éodan, *sv.* 7, *w. dat.* bid, command.
be-b·yrgan, *wv.* bury.
béc, *see* **bóc.**
be-c·lyppan, *wv.* embrace, encompass, hold.
be-c·uman, *sv.* 4, come.
*ge*b·**ed,** *sn.* prayer [biddan].
be-d·ǽlan, *wv. w. gen.* deprive of [dǽl].
będd, *sn.* bed.
be-d·elfan, *sv.* 3. (hide by digging), bury.
*ge*b·**ed-hús,** *sn.* oratory, chapel.
be-f·æstan, *wv.* (make fast); *w. dat.* commit, entrust to.
be-f·oran, *prp. w. dat.* before.
begen, *prn.* both.
be-g·eondan, *prp. w. acc.* beyond.
be-g·ietan, *sv.* 5, get, obtain.
be-g·innan, *sv.* 3, begin.
be-h·átan, *sv.* 1, *w. dat.* promise.
be-h·éafdian, *wv.* behead [héafod].
be-h·ealdan, *sv.* 1, behold.
be-h·ófian, *wv. w. gen.* require.
be-h·réowsian, *wv.* repent [hréowan].
be-h·ýdan, *wv.* hide.
be-l·ǽwan, *wv.* betray.
be-l·íefan, *wv.* believe.
be-l·ífan, *sv.* 6, remain [láf].
be-l·úcan, *sv.* 7, lock, close.
bęnd, *smfn.* bond [bindan].
béodan, *sv.* 7, *w. dat.* offer.
béon, *v.* be—béon ymbe, have to do with.
beorg, *sm.* hill, mountain.
*ge***beorgan,** *sv.* 3, *w. dat.* save, protect.
beornan, *sv.* 3, burn, *intrans.*
béot-lic, *aj.* boastful.
be-p·ǽcan, *wv.* deceive.
beran, *sv.* 4, bear, carry; (geberan, bring forth).
bęrn, *sn.* barn.
berstan, *sv.* 3, burst.
be-s·árgian, *wv.* lament [sárig].
be-s·cieran, *sv.* 4, shear, cut hair.
be-s·éon, *sv.* 5, see, look.
be-s·ęttan, *wv.* set about, surround, cover.
be-s·tealcian, *wv.* go stealthily, steal.
be-s·wícan, *sv.* 6, deceive, circumvent, betray.
be-t·ǽcan, *wv.* commit, entrust, give up.
bętera, bętst, *see* **gód.**
bet·wéonan, *prp. w. dat.* between, among.
be-t·wix, *prep. w. acc. and dat.* between, among; *of time,* during—betwix þám þe, *cj.* while.
be-w·ęrian, *wv.* defend.
be-w·itan, *swv.* watch over, have charge of.
bídan, *sv.* 6, wait.
biddan, *sv.* 5, ask, beg.
*ge*b·**iddan,** *sv.* 5. *refl.* pray.

bieldo, *sf.* (boldness), arrogance [beald].
bíg-gęng, *sm.* worship [big, by, *and* gęng *from* gán].
bile-wit, *aj.* simple, innocent.
bindan, *sv.* 3, bind.
binnan, *av.* inside; *prp. w. dat.* within, in [= be-innan].
biscop, *sm.* bishop [*Latin* episcopus].
bi-smer, *snm.* insult, ignominy.
bismer-full, *aj.* ignominious, shameful.
bismrian, *wv.* treat with ignominy, insult [bismer].
bítan, *sv.* 6, bite.
biþ, *see* **béon**.
bláwan, *sv.* 1, blow.
bleoh, *sn.* colour.
bléow, *see* **bláwan**.
blétsian, *wv.* bless.
blind, *aj.* blind.
bliss, *sf.* merriment, joy.
blissian, *wv.* rejoice.
blíþe, *aj.* glad, merry.
blíþe-lice, *av.* gladly.
blód, *sn.* blood.
bóc, *sf.* book, scripture.
Bóc-læden, *sn.* book Latin, Latin.
bodian, *sm.* announce, preach [béodan].
bodig, *sm.* body.
bohte, *see* **bycgan**.
brád, *aj.* broad.
bræþ, *sm.* vapour, odour.
brecan, *sv.* 4, break; take (city).
bregdan, *sv.* 3, pull.
brémel, *sm.* bramble.
Breten, *sf.* Britain.
Brettas, *smpl.* the British.
Brettisc, *aj.* British [Brettas].
bringan, *wv.* bring.
bróhte, *see* **bringan**.
bróþor, *sm.* brother.
brúcan, *sv.* 7, *w. gen.* enjoy, partake of.
brýd, *sf.* bride.
brýd-guma, *sm.* bridegroom [*literally* bride-man].
búan, *wv.* dwell.
búend, *smpl.* dwellers [*pres. partic. of* búan].
bufan, *prp. w. dat. and acc.* over, above, on.
búgan, *sv.* 7, bend, incline.
bundon, *see* **bindan**.
burg, *sf.* city.
burg-geat, *sn.* city-gate.
bútan, *av.* outside; *prp. w. dat.* without, except, besides [= be-útan].
bútan, *cj.* unless, except.
bycgan, *wv.* buy.
byrþen, *sf.* burden [beran].
byrgen, *sf.* tomb [bebyrgan].
***ge*byrian**, *wf.* be due, befit.
byrig, *see* **burg**.
byrst, *sf.* bristle.
***ge*b·ysnian**. *wv.* give example, illustrate.
***ge*b·ysnung**, *sf.* example.

C.

Cann, *see* **cunnan**.
canón, *sm.* canon; canónes béc, canonical books.
Cantwara-burg, *sf.* Canterbury [Cantwara, *gen. of* Cantware].
Cant-ware, *pl.* Kent-dwellers, men of Kent [*Lat.* Cantia *and* ware].
cásere, *sm.* emperor [*Latin* Caesar].
ceaflas, *smpl.* jaws.
ceald, *aj.* cold.
cealf, *sn.* calf.
céap, *sn.* purchase.
céas, *see* **céosan**.
ceaster, *sf.* city (*Latin* castra).
céne, *aj.* brave, bold.
cęnnan, *wv.* bring forth, bear child.
Cęnt, *sf.* (?) Kent [Cantia].
Cęnt-land, *sn.* Kent.
ceorfan, *sv.* 3, cut.
céosan, *sv.* 7, choose.
cépan, *wv.* attend, look out for.
cíepan, *wv.* trade, sell [céap].
cíepend, *sm.* seller [*pres. partic. of* cíepan].
cierr, *sm.* turn.

cierran, *wv.* turn, return, go—cierran tó, take to.
gec·**ierred-nes**, *sf.* conversion.
cild, *sn.* child.
cild-hád, *sm.* childhood.
cinn-bán, *sn.* jaw-bone.
cirice, *sf.* church.
cléne, *aj.* clean, pure.
clawu, *sf.* claw.
clipian, *wv.* call, summon.
clipung, *sf.* calling.
clyppan, *wv.* clip, embrace.
cnapa, *sm.* (boy, youth) servant.
cnoll, *sm.* top, summit.
coccel, *sm.* corn-cockle.
cóm, *see* **cuman**.
coren, *see* **céosan**.
cræft, *sm.* skill, cunning.
cristen, *aj.* Christian.
cuma, *sm.* stranger [cuman].
cuman, *sv.* 4, come; cuman upp, land.
cunnan, *swv.* know.
cunnian, *wv.* try [cunnan].
curon, *see* céosan.
cúþ, *aj.* known [*originally past partic. of* cunnan].
cwǽdon, *see* **cweþan**.
cwæþ, *see* **cweþan**.
cweartern, *sn.* prison.
cwéman, *wv.* please, gratify.
gec·**wémednes**, *sf.* pleasing.
cwén, *sf.* queen.
cweþan, *sv.* 5, say, speak; name, call.
cwic, *aj.* alive.
cwide, *sm.* speech, address [cweþan].
*ge*c**wid-rǽden**, *sf.* agreement.
cwiþþ, *see* **cweþan**.
cymþ, *see* **cuman**.
cyne-cynn, *sn.* royal family.
cyne-lic, *aj.* royal.
cynelice, *av.* like a king, royally.
cyne-stól, *sm.* throne.
cyning, *sm.* king.
cynn, *sn.* race, kind.
cyst, *sf.* excellence [céosan].
cystig, *aj.* (excellent), charitable.
cýþan, *wv.* make known, tell [cúþ].

D.

Dǽd, *sf.* deed.
dæg, *sm.* day.
dæg-hwám-lice, *av.* daily.
dǽl, *sm.* part—be healfum dǽle, by half.
dǽlan, *wv.* divide, share.
déad, *aj.* dead.
déaþ, *sm.* death.
Defena-scír, *sf.* Devonshire [Devonia].
dehter, *see* **dohtor**.
*ge*d**elf**, *sn.* digging.
delfan, *sv.* 3, dig.
Dęne, *smpl.* Danes.
Dęnisc, *aj.* Danish.
déofol, *snm.* devil [*Latin* diabolus].
déofol-gield, *sn.* idol.
déop, *aj.* deep.
déor, *sn.* wild beast.
déore, *aj.* dear, precious.
déor-wierþe, *aj.* precious.
díegol, *aj.* hidden, secret.
díegol-nes, *sf.* secret.
díepe, *sf.* depth [déop].
dihtan, *wv.* appoint [*Latin* dictare].
disc-þegn, *sm.* (dish-thane), waiter.
dohtor, *sf.* daughter.
dóm, *sm.* doom, judgment, sentence.
dón, *sv.* do, act.
dorste, *see* **durran**.
draca, *sm.* dragon.
dranc, *see* **drincan**.
dréorig, *aj.* sad.
drífan, *sv.* 6, drive.
drinca, *sm.* drink.
drincan, *sv.* 3, drink.
drohtnian, *wv.* live, continue, behave.
drohtnung, *sf.* conduct.
drýge, *aj.* dry.
dún, *sf.* hill, down.
durran, *swv.* dare.
duru, *sf.* door.
dúst, *sn.* dust.
ged·**wyld**, *sn.* error.
dyde, *see* **dón**.
dyppan, *wv.* dip.
dysig, *aj.* foolish.

E.

Éac, *av.* also; éac swelce, also.
éacnian, *wv.* increase.
éadig, *aj.* (prosperous), blessed.
éage, *sn.* eye.
éag-þyrel, *sn.* (eye-hole), window.
eahta, *num.* eight.
éa-lá, *interj.* oh!
eald, *aj.* old—*cp.* ieldra.
Eald-seaxe, *smpl.* Old Saxons.
ealdor, *sm.* chief, master.
ealdor-mann, *sm.* chief, officer.
eall, *aj.* all.
eall, *av.* quite; eall swá micel swá, (quite) as much as.
eall-niwe, *aj.* quite new.
eallunga, *av.* entirely.
ealu, *sn.* ale.
eard, *sm.* country, native land.
eardian, *wv.* dwell.
earm, *sm.* arm.
earm, *aj.* poor, wretched, despicable.
earm-lic, *aj.* miserable.
earm-lice, *av.* miserably, wretchedly.
earn, *sm.* eagle.
eart, *see* **wesan.**
éast, *av.* eastwards.
éast-dǽl, *sm.* east part, the East.
Éast-ęngle, *smpl.* East-Anglians.
Éast-seaxe, *smpl.* East-Saxons.
éaþe-lic, *aj.* insignificant, weak.
éaþ-médan, *wv.* humble [éaþmód].
éaþ-mód, *aj.* humble.
éce, *aj.* eternal.
éc-nes, *sf.* eternity.
efen, *aj.* even.
ge-efen-lǽcan, *wv.* imitate.
efne, *av.* behold, lo! [efen].
ęfsian, *wv.* clip, shear.
ęft, *av.* again; afterwards, then; back.
ęge, *sm.* fear.
ęgesa, *sm.* fear [ęge].
ęges-lic, *aj.* fearful, awful.
éhtere, *sm.* persecutor.
ele, *sm.* oil.
ęl-þéodig-nes, *sf.* foreign land.
ęnde, *sm.* end.
ęndemes, *av.* together.
ge-ęndian, *wv.* end; die.
ęndlufon, *num.* eleven.
ęndlyfta, *aj.* eleventh.
ge-ęndung, *sf.* ending, end.
ęngel, *sm.* angel [*Latin* angelus].
Ęngla-land, *sn.* England [Ęngla *gen. pl. of* Ęngle].
Ęngle, *smpl.* the English [Angel].
Ęnglisc, *aj.* English—*sn.* English language [Engle].
éode, *see* **gán.**
éom, *see* **wesan.**
eorl, *sm.* earl.
eorþ-búend, *sm.* earth-dweller.
eorþe, *sf.* earth.
eorþ-fæst, *aj.* firm in the earth.
eorþ-lic, *aj.* earthly.
eornost, *sf.* earnest.
eornost-lice, *av.* in truth, indeed.
éow, *see* **þú.**
etan, *sv.* 5, eat.
éþel, *sm.* country, native land.

F.

Fæder, *sm.* father.
fægen, *aj.* glad.
fæger, *aj.* fair.
fæger-nes, *sf.* fairness, beauty.
fægnian, *wv. w. gen.* rejoice.
fǽmne, *sf.* virgin.
fǽr, *sf.* danger.
fǽr-lic, *aj.* sudden.
fǽr-lice, *av.* suddenly.
fæst, *aj.* fast, firm.
fæstan, *wv.* fast.
fæsten, *sf.* fasting.
fæt, *sn.* vessel.
fág-nes, *sf.* variegation, various colours.
fandian, *wv. w. gen.* try, test, tempt [findan].
faran, *sv.* 2, go.
faru, *sf.* procession, retinue, pomp.
féa, *aj. pl.* few.
ge-féa, *sm.* joy.
feallan, *sv.* 1, fall.
fearr, *sm.* bull; ox.

feax, *sn.* hair of head.
fédan, *wv.* feed [fóda].
fela, *aj. pl. w. gen.* many.
feld, *sm.* field.
feoh, *sn.* money, property.
gef'**eoht**, *sn.* fight.
feohtan, *sv.* 3, fight.
féole, *sf.* file.
féolian, *wv.* file.
féoll, *see* **feallan**.
féond, *sm.* enemy.
feorh, *snm.* life.
feorm, *sf.* (food); feast, banquet.
feorr, *av.* far.
féorþa, *num.* fourth.
féower, *num.* four.
gef'**éra**, *sm.* companion [fór].
féran, *wv.* go, fare [fór].
gef'**éran**, *wv.* (go over), take possession of.
fęrian, *wv.* carry [faran].
fét, *see* **fót**.
fętian, *wv.* fetch—*pret.* gefętte.
gef'**ętte**, *see* **fętian**.
fiend, *see* **féond**.
fierd, *sf.* army [faran].
fierlen, *aj.* distant [feorr].
fierst, *sm.* period, time.
fíf, *num.* five.
findan, *sv* 3 (*pret.* funde), find.
fisc, *sm.* fish.
fisc-cynn, *sn.* fish-kind.
fléam, *sm.* flight [fléon].
fleax, *sn.* flax.
fléogan, *sv.* 7, fly.
fléon, *sv.* 7, flee.
fléotan, *sv.* 7, float.
flítan, *sv.* 6, quarrel, dispute.
gef'**líeman**, *wv.* put to flight [fléam].
flód, *sm.* flood.
flota, *sm.* fleet [fléotan].
flot-hęre, *sm.* naval army, army of pirates.
flot-mann, *sm* sailor, pirate.
flówan, *sv.* 1, flow.
flugon, *see* **fléon**
flyht, *sm.* flight [fléogan].
fóda, *sm.* food.
folc, *sn.* people, nation.
folc-lic, *aj.* popular.
folgian, *wv. w. dat.* follow; obey.
fón, *sv.* 1, seize, take, capture; féng tó ríce, came to the throne; tógædre féngon, joined together.
for, *prep. w. dat.* before—ríce for worulde, in the eyes of the world; *causal*, for, because of, for the sake of—ne dorste for Gode, for the fear of God—for þám, therefore, for þám (þe), because; *w. acc.*, instead of, for.
fór, *sf.* journey [faran].
fór, *see* **faran**.
for-b'**ærnan**, *wv.* burn up, burn, *trans.*
for-b'**éodan**, *sv.* 7, forbid.
for-b'**réotan**, *sv.* 7, break.
for-c'**eorfan**, *sv.* 3, cut off.
for-d'**ilgian**, *wv.* destroy.
for-d'**ón**, *sv.* destroy.
for-e'**aldod**, *aj.* aged [*past partic. of* forealdian, grow old].
fore-scéawian, *wv.* pre-ordain, decree, appoint.
fore-sęcgan, *wv.* say before—se foresægda, the aforesaid.
for-g'**iefan**, *sv.* 5, *w. dat.* give, grant; forgive.
forg'**ief-nes**, *sf.* forgiveness.
forht, *aj.* afraid.
forhtian, *wv.* be afraid.
for-h'**wega**, *av.* somewhere.
for-l'**ǽtan**, *sv.* 1, leave, abandon.
for-l'**éosan**, *sv.* 7, lose.
for-l'**iger**, *sn.* wantonness, immorality.
forma, *aj.* first—*superl.* fyrmest, first.
for-m'**olsnian**, *wv.* crumble, decay.
for-s'**crincan**, *sv.* 3, shrink up.
for-séon, *sv.* 5, despise.
for-s'**léan**, *sv.* 2, cut through.
for-st'**andan**, *sv.* 2, (stand before), protect.
forþ, *av.* forth, forwards, on.
forþ-f'**éran**, *wv.* depart, die.
for-þ'**rysman**, *wv.* suffocate, choke.
for-w'**eorþan**, *sv.* 3, perish.

fót, *sm.* foot.
frætwian, *wv.* adorn.
frætwung, *sf.* ornament.
fram, *prep. w. dat.* from; *agent. w. pass.* híe wǽron fram Wyrtgeorne gelaþode, invited by.
fręmman, *wv.* perform, do.
fréond, *sm.* friend.
friþ, *sm.* peace—friþ niman, make peace.
fugol, *sm.* bird.
fuhton, *see* **feohtan**.
fúl, *aj.* foul, impure.
full, *aj.* full.
full-b·líþe, *aj.* very glad.
full-c·éne, *aj.* very brave.
ful-lice, *av.* fully.
full-s·óþ, *aj.* very true.
fultum, *sm.* help; forces, troops.
fultumian, *wv. w. dat.* help.
funde, *see* **findan**.
furþor, *av.* further, more [forþ].
fús, *aj.* hastening.
fyllan, *wv.* fill, fulfil [full].
fýr, *sn.* fire.
fyrmest, *see* **forma**.

G.

Gadrian, *wv.* gather.
gærs, *sn.* grass.
gafeloc, *sm.* missile, spear.
gafol, *sn.* interest, profit.
gamen, *sn.* sport.
gán, *sv.* go.
*geg·*án, *sv.* gain, conquer.
gást, *sm.* spirit; se hálga gást, the Holy Ghost.
gást-lic, *aj.* spiritual.
ge, *cj.* and—ge . . ge, both . . and.
gé, *see* **þú**.
gealga, *sm.* gallows.
géar, *sn.* year.
gearcian, *wv.* prepare [gearo].
geard, *sm.* yard, court.
gearo, *aj.* ready.
gearwian, *wv.* prepare.
géoguþ, *sf.* youth.
géomrung, *sf.* lamentation.
geond, *prp. w. acc.* through, throughout.
géong, *aj.* young.
georn, *aj.* eager [giernan].
georne, *av.* eagerly, earnestly.
giefan, *sv.* 5, give.
giefta, *sfpl.* marriage, wedding [giefan].
gieft-hús, *sn.* wedding-hall.
gieft-lic, *aj.* wedding.
giefu, *sf.* gift; grace (of God) [giefan].
giemm, *sm.* gem, jewel [*Latin* gemma].
giem-stán, *sm.* gem, jewel.
gierla, *sm.* dress [gearu].
giernan, *wv. w. gen.* yearn, desire; ask [georn].
giet, *av.* yet; further, besides.
gif, *cj.* if.
git, *see* **þú**.
gítsian, *wv.* covet.
gítsung, *sf.* covetousness, avarice.
glæd, *aj.* glad.
glæd-lice, *av.* gladly.
gléaw, *aj.* prudent, wise.
glęngan, *wv.* adorn; trim (lamp).
god, *sm.* God.
god-fæder, *sm.* godfather.
god-spell, *sn.* gospel.
godspel-lic, *aj.* evangelical.
gód, *aj.* good—*compar.* bętera, *superl.* bętst.
gód, *sn.* good thing, good.
gold, *sn.* gold.
gold-hord, *sn.* treasure.
grǽdig, *aj.* greedy.
grǽg, *aj.* grey.
grétan, *wv.* greet, salute.
grindan, *sv.* 3, grind.
grist-bítung, *sf.* gnashing of teeth.
grymetian, *wv.* grunt, roar.
gyldan, *wv.* gild [gold].
gylden, *aj.* golden [gold].

H.

Habban, *wv.* have; take.
hád, *sm.* rank, condition.

geh·**ǽdod**, *aj.* ordained, in orders, clerical [*past partic. of* hádian, ordain].
hæfde, hæfþ, *see* **habban.**
hæftan, *wv.* hold fast, hold [habban].
hǽlan, *wv.* heal [hál].
hǽlend, *sm.* Saviour [*pres. partic. of* hǽlan].
hǽlo, *sf.* salvation [hál].
hæpse, *sf.* hasp.
hǽs, *sf.* command.
hǽte, *sf.* heat [hát].
hǽþ, *sf.* heath.
hǽþen, *aj.* heathen [hǽþ].
hál, *aj.* whole, sound.
geh·**ál**, *aj.* whole, uninjured.
hálga, *sm.* saint.
hálgian, *wv.* hallow, consecrate.
hálig, *aj.* holy.
hálig-dóm, *sm.* holy object, relic.
hám, *av.* homewards, home.
hand, *sf.* hand.
hand-cweorn, *sf.* hand-mill.
hangian, *wv.* hang, *intr.* [hón].
hát, *aj.* hot.
hátan, *sv.* I, command, ask—*w. inf. in passive sense*, héton him sęcgan, bade them be told; name—*passive*, hátte.
hatian, *wv.* hate.
hátte, *see* **hátan.**
hé, *prn.* he.
héafod, *sn.* head.
héafod-mann, *sm.* head-man, ruler, chief.
héah, *aj.* high—*superl.* híehst.
healdan, *sv.* I, hold, keep; guard; preserve; observe; keep.
healf, *aj.* half.
healf, *sf.* side.
héa-lic, *aj.* lofty [héah].
heall, *sf.* hall.
heard, *aj.* hard; strong; severe.
hębban, *sv.* 2, raise.
hęfel-þrǽd, *sm.* web-thread, thread.
hęfe, *sm.* weight [hębban].
hęfig, *aj.* heavy [hęfe].
geh·**ęnde**, *aj. w. dat.* near [hand].
héo, *see* **hé.**
heofon, *sm.* heaven—*often in plur.*, heofona ríce.
heofon-lic, *aj.* heavenly.
héold, *see* **healdan.**
heord, *sf.* herd.
heorte, *sf.* heart.
hér, *av.* here; hither—héræ·fter, &c., hereafter.
hér-be-é·astan, *av.* east of this.
hęre, *sm.* army.
hęre-réaf, *sn.* spoil.
hęre-toga, *sm.* army-leader, general, chief [toga *from* téon].
hęrgian, *wv.* ravage, make war [hęre].
hęrgung, *sf.* (ravaging), warfare, war.
hęrian, *wv.* praise.
hét, *see* **hátan.**
hider, *av.* hither.
hie, *see* **hé.**
híehst, *see* **héah.**
hiera, *see* **hé.**
geh·**ieran**, *wv.* hear.
hierde, *sm.* shepherd [heord].
hierd-rǽden, *sf.* guardianship.
hiere, *see* **hé.**
geh·**ier-sum**, *aj. w. dat.* obedient [híeran].
geh·**iersum-nes**, *sf.* obedience.
him, hine, *see* **hé.**
híred, *snm.* family, household.
his, *see* **hé.**
hit, *see* **hé.**
hiw, *sn.* hue, form.
hlǽdder, *sf.* ladder.
hlæst, *sm.* load.
hláf, *sm.* bread, loaf of bread.
hláford, *sm.* lord.
hlísa, *sm.* fame.
hlúd, *aj.* loud.
hlýdan, *wv.* make a noise, shout [hlúd].
hnappian, *wv.* doze.
geh·**oferod**, *aj.* (past partic.), hump-backed.
holt, *sn.* wood.
hón, *sv.* I, hang [hangian].

horn, *sm.* horn.
hræd-lice, *av.* quickly.
hrædung, *sf.* hurry.
hraþe, *av.* quickly—swá hraþe swá, as soon as.
hréod, *sn.* reed.
hréowan, *sv.* 7, rue, repent.
hríeman, *wv.* cry, call.
hriþer, *sn.* ox.
hróf, *sn.* roof.
hrycg, *sm.* back.
hryre, *sm.* fall [hréosan].
hú, *av.* how.
hú-meta, *av.* how.
hund, *sn. w. gen.* hundred.
hund, *sm.* dog.
hund-feald, *aj.* hundredfold.
hund-n·igontig, *num.* ninety.
hund-t·węlftig, *num.* hundred and twenty.
hungor, *sm.* hunger; famine.
hungrig, *aj.* hungry.
húru, *av.* especially.
hús, *sn.* house.
hux-lice, *av.* ignominiously.
hwá, *prn.* who.
geh·**wá,** *prn.* every one.
hwǽr, *av.* where—swá hwǽr swá, wherever.
geh·**wǽr,** *av.* everywhere.
hwæs, hwæt, *see* **hwá.**
hwæt, *interj.* what! lo! well.
hwǽte, *sm.* wheat.
hwæþer, *av. cj.* whether—hwæþer þe, *to introduce a direct question.*
hwæþre, *av.* however.
hwane, *see* **hwá.**
hwanne, *av.* when.
hwanon, *av.* whence.
hwelc, *prn.* which; any one, any—swá hwelc swá, whoever.
geh·**welc,** *prn.* any, any one.
hwíl, *sf.* while, time.
hwý, *av.* why.
hýdan, *wv.* hide.
hyht, *sf.* hope.
hyhtan, *wv.* hope.
hýrian, *wv.* hire.

I.

Ic, *prn.* I.
ídel, *aj.* idle; useless, vain—on ídel, in vain.
íeg-land, *sn.* island.
ieldan, *wv.* delay [eald].
ieldra, *see* **eald.**
ieldran, *smpl.* ancestors [*originally compar. of* eald].
iernan, *sv.* 3, run; flow.
ierre, *aj.* angry.
íl, *sm.* hedgehog.
ilca, *prn.* same (always weak, and with the definite article).
in, *prp. w. dat. and acc.* in, into.
inc, *see* **þú.**
inn, *av.* in (of motion).
innan, *prp. w. dat.* (*av.*) within.
inne, *av.* within, inside.
inn-gehygd, *sn.* inner thoughts, mind.
in-tó, *prp. w. dat.* into.
Iotan, *smpl.* Jutes.
Ír-land, *sn.* Ireland.
Iudeisc, *aj.* Jewish—þá Iudeiscan, the Jews.

L.

Lá, *interj.* lo!—lá léof! Sir!
lác, *sn.* gift; offering, sacrifice.
gel·**ǽcean,** *wv.* seize.
lǽdan, *wv.* lead; carry, bring, take.
læden, *sn.* Latin; language [Latina (lingua)].
læg, *see* **licgan.**
lǽran, *wv. w. double acc.* teach; advise, suggest [lár].
gel·**ǽred,** *aj.* learned [*past partic. of* lǽran].
læs, *av.* less— þý læs (þe), *cj. w. subj.* lest.
lǽtan, *sv.* 1, let; leave—héo lét þá swá, she let the matter rest there.
gel·**ǽte,** *sn.*—wega gelǽtu, *pl.* meetings of the roads.
láf, *sf.* remains—tó láfe béon, remain over, be left [(be)lífan].

*ge*l·**amp**, *see ge***limpan.**
land, *sn.* land, country.
land-folc, *sn.* people of the country.
land-hęre, *sm.* land-army.
land-léode, *smpl.* people of the country.
lang, *aj.* long.
lange, *av.* for a long time, long.
lang-lice, *av.* for a long time, long.
lár, *sf.* teaching, doctrine.
late, *av.* slowly, late—late on géare, late in the year.
*ge*l·**aþian,** *wv.* invite.
*ge*l·**aþung,** *sf.* congregation.
léaf, *sf.* leave.
*ge*l·**éafa,** *sm.* belief, faith.
*ge*l·**éaf-full,** *aj.* believing, pious.
leahtor, *sm.* crime, vice.
léas, *aj.* without (expers), *in compos.* -less; false.
léat, *see* **lútan.**
lęcgan, *wv.* lay [licgan].
*ge*l·**ęndan,** *wv.* land [land].
léo, *smf.* lion.
léode, *smpl.* people.
léof, *aj.* dear, beloved; pleasant—mé wǽre léofre, I would rather—[lufu].
leofode, *see* **libban.**
léoht, *sn.* light.
léoht-fæt, *sn.* (light-vessel), lamp.
leornian, *wv.* learn.
leornung-cniht, *sm.* disciple.
lét, *see* **lǽtan.**
libban, *wv.* live.
líc, *sn.* body, corpse.
*ge*l·**íc,** *aj. w. dat.* like.
*ge*l·**íce,** *av.* in like manner, alike, equally.
licgan, *sv.* 5, lie.
líc-hama, *sm.* body.
lícham-lice, *av.* bodily.
*ge***lícian,** *wv. w. dat.* please.
líefan, *wv. w. dat.* allow [léaf].
*ge*l·**íefan,** *wv.* believe [geléafa].
líf, *sn.* life.
lim, *sn.* limb, member.
*ge*l·**imp,** *sn.* event, emergency, calamity.
*ge*l·**impan,** *sv.* 3, happen.
líþ, *see* **licgan.**
locc, *sm.* lock of hair.
lof, *sn.* praise; glory.
*ge*l·**ógian,** place; occupy, furnish.
*ge*l·**óm,** *aj.* frequent, repeated.
*ge*l·**óme,** *av.* often, repeatedly.
losian, *wv. w. dat.* be lost—him losaþ, he loses [(for)léosan].
lúcan, *sv.* 7, close.
lufu, *sf.* love [léof].
Lunden-burg, *sf.* London [Lundonia].
lútan, *sv.* 7, stoop.
lytel, *aj.* little.

M.

Má, *see* **micel.**
macian, *wv.* make.
mæg, *see* **mugan.**
mægen, *sn.* strength, capacity; virtue [mugan].
mǽgþ, *sf.* family; tribe, nation; generation.
*ge*m·**ǽne,** *aj.* common.
*ge*m·**ǽnelic,** *aj.* common, general.
mǽre, *aj.* famous, glorious, great (metaphorically).
*ge*m·**ǽre,** *sn.* boundary, territory.
mǽrsian, *wv.* extol, celebrate [mǽre].
mǽrþo, *sf.* glory [mǽre].
mæsse, *sf.* mass [*Latin* missa].
mæsse-préost, *sm.* mass-priest.
mǽst, *see* **micel.**
magon, *see* **mugan.**
man, *indef.* one [mann].
mán, *sn.* wickedness.
mán-dǽd, *sf.* wicked deed.
mán-full, *aj.* wicked.
mangere, *sm.* merchant.
mangung, *sf.* trade, business.
manig, *aj.* many.
manig-feald, *aj.* manifold.
manig-fieldan, *wv.* multiply [manigfeald].
mann, *sm.* man; person.
mann-cynn, *sn.* mankind.

mann-rǽden, *sf.* allegiance.
mann-slaga, *sm.* manslayer, murderer [sléan, slęge].
máre, *see* **micel**.
martyr, *sm.* martyr.
máþm, *sm.* treasure.
máþm-fæt, *sn.* precious vessel.
mé, *see* **ic**.
mearc, *sf.* boundary.
méd, *sf.* reward, pay.
méder, *see* **módor**.
męnn, *see* **mann**.
męnnisc, *aj.* human [mann].
męre-grot, *sn.* pearl [margarita].
mergen, *sm.* morning [morgen].
gem·**et**, *sn.* measure; manner, way.
metan, *sv.* 5, measure.
gem·**étan**, *wv.* meet; find [gemót].
męte, *sm.* food—*pl.* męttas.
micel, *aj.* great, much—*compar.* máre, má (*adv.*), *superl.* mǽst.
micle, *av.* greatly, much.
mid, *prp. w. dat.* (*instr.*) with—mid þám þe, *cj.* when.
middan-geard, *sm.* world [*literally* middle enclosure].
midde, *aj.* mid, middle (only of time).
middel, *sn.* middle.
Middel-ęngle, *smpl.* Middle-Angles.
Mierce, *smpl.* Mercians [mearc].
miht, *sf.* might, strength; virtue [mugan].
mihte, *see* **mugan**.
mihtig, *aj.* mighty, strong.
míl, *sf.* mile [*Latin* milia (passuum)].
mild-heort, *aj.* mild-hearted, merciful.
gem·**iltsian**, *wv. w. dat.* have mercy on, pity [milde].
mín, *see* **ic**.
mis-lǽdan, *wv.* mislead, lead astray.
mis-lic, *aj.* various.
mód, *sn.* heart, mind.
módig, *aj.* proud.
módig-nes, *sf.* pride.
módor, *sf.* mother.
molde, *sf.* mould, earth.
móna, *sm.* moon.
mónaþ, *sm.* month—*pl.* mónaþ [móna].
morgen, *sm.* morning.
morþ, *sn.* (murder), crime.
móste, *see* **mótan**.
gem·**ót**, *sn.* meeting.
mótan, *swv.* may; ne mót, must not.
mugan, *swv.* can, be able.
gem·**unan**, *swv.* remember.
munt, *sm.* mountain, hill [*Latin* montem].
munuc, *sm.* monk [*Latin* monachus].
murcnian, *wv.* grumble, complain.
múþ, *sm.* mouth.
múþa, *sm.* mouth of a river [múþ].
gem·**ynd**, *sf.* memory, mind [gemunan].
gem·**yndig**, *aj. w. gen.* mindful.
mynet, *sf.* coin [*Latin* moneta].
mynetere, *sm.* money-changer.
mynster, *sn.* monastery [*Latin* monasterium].

N.

Ná, *av.* not, no [=ne á].
næbban = ne habban.
nǽddre, *sf.* snake.
næfde, **næfst**, = ne hæfde, ne hæfst.
nǽfre, *av.* never [=ne ǽfre].
nægel, *sm.* nail.
næs = ne wæs.
náht, *prn. w. gen.* naught, nothing [=nán wiht].
náht-nes, *sf.* worthlessness, cowardice.
nam, *see* **niman**.
nama, *sm.* name.
námon, *see* **niman**.
nán, *prn.* none, no [=ne án].
nát = ne wát.
náwþer, *prn.* neither [=ne áhwæþer (either)].
ne, *av.* not—ne . . ne, neither . . not.

néah, *av.* near; *superl.* níehst—æt níehstan, next, immediately, afterwards.
nearo, *aj.* narrow.
néa-wist, *sfm.* neighbourhood [wesan].
nęmnan, *wv.* name [nama].
néom = ne eom.
nese, *av.* no.
nętt, *sn.* net.
níed, *sf.* need.
níedunga, *av.* needs, by necessity.
níęhst, *see* **néah**.
níeten, *sn.* animal.
nigon, *num.* nine.
nigoþa, *aj.* ninth.
niht, *sf.* night.
niman, *sv.* 4, take, capture; take in marriage, marry.
nis = ne is.
niþer, *av.* down.
niwe, *aj.* new.
gen·**óg**, *aj.* enough.
nolde = ne wolde.
norþ, *av.* north.
Norþhymbra-land, *sn.* Northumberland.
Norþ-hymbre, *smpl.* Northumbrians [Humbra].
norþan-weard, *aj.* northward.
Norþ-męnn, *pl.* Norwegians.
nú, *av.* now, just now; *cj. causal*, now that, since.
nú-g·iet, *av.* still.
geny·**ht-sum-nes**, *sf.* sufficience, abundance.
nyle, = ne wile.
nyste, **nyton** = ne wiste, ne witon.

O.

Of, *prp. w. dat.* of, from *of place, origin, privation, release*, &c.; *partitive*, sęllaþ ús of éowrum ele, some of your oil.
of-d·rǽdd, *aj.* afraid [*past partic. of* ofdrǽdan, dread].
ofer, *prp. w. dat. and acc.* over; on; *of time*, during, throughout, over.
ofer-gyld, *aj.* (past partic.), gilded over, covered with gold.
ofer·hęrgian, *wv.* ravage, overrun.
ofer-s·áwan, *sv.* 2, sow over.
offrian, *wv.* offer, sacrifice [*Latin* offerre].
offrung, *sf.* offering, sacrifice.
of-s·léan, *sv.* 2, slay.
of-s·níþan, *sv.* 6, kill [sníþan, 'cut'].
of-spring, *sm.* offspring [springan].
oft, *av.* often.
of-téon, *sv.* 7, *w. dat. of pers. and gen. of thing*, deprive.
of-þ·yrst, *aj.* thirsty [*past partic. of* ofþyrstan, *from* þurst].
of-w·undrian, *wv. w. gen.* wonder.
ó-lǽcung, *sf.* flattery.
olfend, *sm.* camel [*Latin* elephas].
on, *prp. w. dat. and acc.* on; in; *hostility*, against, on híe fuhton; *of time*, in.
on-b·yrgan, *wv.* taste.
on-c·náwan, *sv.* 1, know, recognize.
on-f·ón, *sv.* 1, receive.
on-g·éan, *prp. w. dat. and acc.* towards; *hostility*, against.
on-g·éan, *av.* back—gewęnde ongéan, returned.
on-ginn, *sn.* beginning.
on-g·innan, *sv.* 3, begin.
on-l·íehtan, *wv.* illuminate, enlighten [léoht].
onl·íehtung, *sf.* illumination, light.
on-l·úcan, *sv.* 7, unlock.
on-m·iddan, *prp. w. dat.* in the midst of.
on-síen, *sf.* appearance, form.
on-sund, *aj.* sound, whole.
on-u·ppan, *prp. w. dat.* upon.
on-weald, *sm* rule, authority, power; territory.
on-w·eg, *av.* away.
open, *aj.* open.
openian, *wv.* open, reveal, disclose.
orgel-lice, *av.* proudly.

or-mǽte, *aj.* immense, boundless [metan].
or-sorg, *aj.* unconcerned, careless.
óþ, *prp. w. acc.* until—óþ þæt, *cj.* until; up to, as far as.
óþer, *prn.* (always strong), second; other.
oþþe, *cj.* or—oþþe . . oþþe, either . . or.
oxa, *sm.* ox.

P.

Pápa, *sm.* pope [*Latin* papa].
pęning, *sm.* penny.
Peohtas, *smpl.* Picts.
Philisteisc, *aj.* Philistine.
Pihtisc, *aj.* Pictish [Peohtas].
plegian, *wv.* play.
post, *sm.* post [*Latin* postis].
préost, *sm.* priest [*Latin* presbyter].
pund, *sn.* pound [*Latin* pondus].
pytt, *sm.* pit [*Latin* puteus].

R.

Racentéag, *sf.* chains.
rád, *see* **rídan**.
*ge*r·**ád**, *sn.* reckoning, account; on þá gerád þæt, on condition that.
rǽd, *sm.* advice; what is advisable, plan of action—him rǽd þúhte, it seemed advisable to him.
ramm, *sm.* ram.
ráp, *sm.* rope.
réaf, *sn.* robe, dress.
reahte, *see* **reccan**.
récan, *wv. w. gen.* reck, care.
ręccan, *wv.* tell, narrate.
*ge*r·**accednes**, *sf.* narrative.
*ge*r·**ǽfa**, *sm.* officer, reeve, bailiff.
regen, *sm.* rain.
réþe, *aj.* fierce, cruel.
ríce, *aj.* powerful, of high rank.
ríce, *sn.* kingdom, sovereignty, government.
ríceтere, *sn.* (ambition), pomp.
rícsian, *wv.* rule.
rídan, *sv.* 6, ride.
riftere, *sm.* reaper.
riht, *aj.* right; righteous.
riht-líce, *av.* rightly, correctly.
riht-wísnes, *sf.* righteousness.
rím, *sm.* number.
ríman, *wv.* count.
rínan, *wv.* rain [regen].
rípan, *sv.* 6, reap.
rípere, *sm.* reaper.
ríp-tíma, *sm.* reaping-time, harvest.
róhte, *see* **récan**.
Róme-burg, *sf.* city of Rome.
rówan, *sv.* 1, row.
ryne, *sm.* course.
*ge*r·**ýne**, *sn.* mystery.

S.

Sǽ, *sf.* sea—*dat.* sǽ.
sǽd, *sn.* seed.
sægde, *see* **sęcgan**.
sǽl, *sm.* time, occasion.
*ge*s·**ǽlig**, *aj.* happy, blessed.
*ge*s·**ǽlig-líce**, *av.* happily, blessedly.
sæt, **sǽton**, *see* **sittan**.
sagol, *sm.* rod, staff.
*ge*s·**amnian**, *wv.* collect, assemble.
samod, *av.* together, with.
sanct, *sm.* saint [*Latin* sanctus].
sand, *sf.* dish of food [sęndan].
sand-ceosol, *sm.* sand (*literally* sand-gravel).
sár, *sn.* grief.
sár, *aj.* grievous.
sárig, *aj.* sorry, sad.
sáwan, *sv.* 1, sow.
sáwere, *sm.* sower.
sáwol, *sf.* soul.
scamu, *sf.* shame.
scand, *sf.* disgrace.
scand-líc, *aj.* shameful.
scéaf, *sm.* sheaf [scúfan].
scéaf-mǽlum, *av.* sheafwise.
*ge*sc·**eaft**, *sf.* creature, created thing.
sceal, *see* **sculan**.
scéap, *sn.* sheep.
sceatt, *sm.* (tribute); money.
scéawere, *sm.* spy, witness.
scéawian, *wv.* see; examine; read.
scéawung, *sf.* seeing, examination.

scéotan, *sv.* 7, shoot.
scieppan, *sv.* 2, create.
scieran, *sv.* 4, shear.
scip, *sn.* ship.
scip-hęre, *sm.* fleet.
scip-hlæst, *sm.* (shipload), crew.
scír, *sf.* shire.
scolde, *see* **sculan**.
scóp, *see* **scieppan**.
scort, *aj.* short.
scotian, *wv.* shoot [scéotan].
Scot-land, *sn.* Ireland.
Scottas, *smpl.* the Irish.
scotung, *sf.* shot.
scræf, *sn.* cave.
scrín, *sn.* shrine [*Latin* scrinium].
scrincan, *sv.* 3, shrink.
scrúd, *sn.* dress.
scrýdan, *wv.* clothe [scrúd].
scúfan, *sv.* 7, push—scúfan út, launch (ship).
sculan, *swv.* ought to, must; shall.
scuton, *see* **scéotan**.
scyld, *sf.* guilt [sculan].
scyldig, *aj.* guilty.
scylen, *see* **sculan**.
Scyttisc, *aj.* Scotch [Scottas].
se, *prn.* that; the; he: who.
*ge*seah, *see* *ge*séon.
sealde, *see* **sęllan**.
séaþ, *sm.* pit.
Seaxe, *smpl.* Saxons.
sécan, *wv.* seek; visit, come to; attack.
sęcgan, *wv.* say.
self, *prn.* self.
sęllan, *wv.* give; sell.
sélost, *av. superl.* best.
sęndan, *wv.* send, send message.
séo, *see* **se**.
seofon, *num.* seven.
seofoþa, *aj.* seventh.
seolc, *sf.* silk.
seolcen, *aj.* silken.
seolfor, *sn.* silver.
*ge*s·éon, *sv.* 5, see.
séow, *see* **sáwan**.
*ge*s·ętnes, *sf.* narrative [sęttan].
sęttan, *wv.* set; appoint, institute—dóm sęttan *w. dat.* pass sentence on; compose, write; create [sittan].
sibb, *sf.* peace.
*ge*s·ibb-sum, *aj.* peaceful.
síe, *see* **wesan**.
siefer-lice, *av.* purely.
síefre, *aj.* pure.
sierwung, *sf.* stratagem.
siex, *num.* six.
siexta, *aj.* sixth.
siextig, *num.* sixty.
siextig-feald, *aj.* sixtyfold.
sige, *sm.* victory—sige niman, gain the victory.
sige-fæst, *aj.* victorious.
*ge*s·ihþ, *sf.* sight; vision, dream [geséon].
silfren, *aj.* silver.
simle, *av.* always.
sind, *see* **wesan**.
sinu, *sf.* sinew.
sittan, *sv.* 5, sit; settle, stay.
*ge*s·ittan, *sv.* 5, take possession of.
síþ, *sm.* journey.
síþian, *wv.* journey, go.
siþþan, *av.* since, afterwards; *cj.* when.
slǽp, *sm.* sleep.
slǽpan, *sv.* 1, sleep.
slaga, *sm.* slayer [sléan, *past partic.* geslægen].
sláw, *aj.* slow, slothful, dull.
sléan, *sv.* 2, strike; slay, kill.
slęcg, *sm.* hammer [slaga, sléan].
slęge, *sm.* killing [slaga, sléan].
slép, *see* **slǽpan**.
slóg, *see* **sléan**.
smæl, *aj.* narrow.
sméan, *wv.* consider, think; consult.
sméocan, *sv.* 7, smoke.
sméþe, *aj.* smooth.
snotor, *aj.* wise, prudent.
sóna, *av.* soon; then.
sorg, *sf.* sorrow.
sóþ, *aj.* true.
sóþ, *sn.* truth.
sóþ-lice, *av.* truly, indeed.

spadu, *sf.* spade [*Latin* spatha].
spræc, *sf.* speech, language; conversation [sprecan].
sprecan, *sv.* 5, speak.
spręngan, *wv.* (scatter); sow [springan].
springan, *sv.* 3, spring.
sprungen, *see* **springan**.
stǽnen, *aj.* of stone [stán].
stǽniht, *sn.* stony ground [*originally adj.* 'stony,' from stán].
stán, *sm.* stone; brick.
standan, *sv.* 2, stand.
stéap, *aj.* steep.
stęde, *sm.* place.
stefn, *sf.* voice.
stelan, *sv.* 4, steal.
stęnt, *see* **standan**.
stéor, *sf.* steering, rudder.
steorra, *sm.* star.
sticol, *aj.* rough.
stíepel, *sm.* steeple [stéap].
stíeran, *wv. w. dat.* restrain [stéor].
ges·**tillan**, *wv.* stop, prevent.
stille, *aj.* still, quiet.
stód, *see* **standan**.
stól, *sm.* seat.
stów, *sf.* place.
strǽt, *sf.* street, road [*Latin* strata via].
strand, *sm.* shore.
strang, *aj.* strong.
strédan, *wv.* (scatter), sow.
stręngþo, *sf.* strength [strang].
ges·**tréon**, *sn.* possession.
ges·**tríenan**, *wv.* gain [gestréon].
strútian, *wv.* strut.
stycce, *sn.* piece.
sum, *prn.* some, a certain (one), one; a.
ges·**und**, *aj.* sound, healthy.
ges·**und-full**, *aj.* safe and sound.
sundor, *av.* apart.
sunne, *sf.* sun.
sunu, *sm.* son.
súþ, *av.* south, southwards.
súþan, *av.* from the south.
súþan-weard, *aj.* southward.
súþ-dæl, *sm.* the South.
súþerne, *aj.* southern.
Súþ-seaxe, *smpl.* South-saxons.
swá, *av.* so; swá, swá, as, like—swá . . swá, so . . as.
swác, *see* **swícan**.
swá-þ·éah, *av.* however.
swefn, *sn.* sleep; dream.
swelc, *prn.* such.
swelce, *av.* as if, as it were, as, like.
sweltan, *sv.* 3, die.
swęncan, *wv.* afflict, molest [swincan].
swęng, *sm.* stroke, blow [swingan].
sweor, *sm.* pillar.
sweora, *sm.* neck.
sweord, *sn.* sword.
sweord-bora, *sm.* sword-bearer [beran].
sweotolian, *wv.* display, show, indicate.
sweotolung, *sf.* manifestation, sign.
swęrian, *sv.* 2, swear.
swic, *sm.* deceit.
ges·**wícan**, *sv.* 6 (fail, fall short); cease (betray).
swíc-dóm, *sm.* deceit [swícan].
swicol, *aj.* deceitful, treacherous.
swicon, *see* **swícan**.
swift, *aj.* swift.
swígian, *wv.* be silent.
swincan, *sv.* 3, labour, toil.
swingan, *sv.* 3, beat.
swingle, *sf.* stroke [swingan].
swipe, *sm.* whip.
swíþe, *av.* very, much, greatly, violently—*cp.* swíþor, rather, more.
swíþ-lic, *aj.* excessive, great.
swíþre, *sf.* right hand [*cp. of* swíþe *with* hand *understood*].
swulton, *see* **sweltan**.
swuncon, *see* **swincan**.
swungon, *see* **swingan**.
syndrig, *aj.* separate [sundor].
syn-full, *aj.* sinful.
syngian, *wv.* sin.
synn, *sf.* sin.

T.

Tácen, *sn*. sign, token; miracle.
tácnian, *wv*. signify.
get·**ácnung**, *sf*. signification, type.
tǽcan, *wv*. *w*. *dat*. show ; teach.
talu, *sf*. number [getel].
tam, *aj*. tame.
tawian, *wv*. ill-treat.
téam, *sm*. progeny [téon].
get·**el**, *sn*. number.
tęllan, *wv*. count, account—tęllan tó náhte, count as naught [talu].
Tęmes, *sf*. Thames [Tamisia].
tempel, *sn*. temple [*Latin* templum].
téon, *sv*. 7, pull, drag.
téona, *sm*. injury, insult.
téon-rǽden, *sf*. humiliation.
téþ, *see* **tóþ**.
ticcen, *sn*. kid.
tíd, *sf*. time ; hour.
tíegan, *wv*. tie.
tíeman, *wv*. teem, bring forth [téam].
tíen, *num*. ten.
tierwe, *sf*. tar.
tigele, *wf*. tile [*Latin* tegula].
timbrian, *wv*. build.
get·**imbrung**, *sf*. building.
tintreg, *sn*. torture.
tintregian, *wv*. torture.
tó, *prp*. *w*. *dat*. (*av*.) to—tó abbode gesętt, made abbot ; *time*, at—tó langum fierste, for a long time; *adverbial*, tó scande, ignominiously ; *fitness*, *purpose*, *for*—þǽm folce (dat.) tó déaþe, to the death of the people, so that the people were killed; tó þám þæt, *cj*. in order that—tó þám (swíþe) . . þæt, so (greatly) . . that.
tó, *av*. too.
tó-b·**erstan**, *sv*. 3, burst, break asunder.
tó-b·**recan**, *sv*. 4, break in pieces, break through.
tó-b·**regdan**, *sv*. 3, shake off, cast off.
tó-c·**wíesan**, *wv*. crush, bruise.
tó-cyme, *sm*. coming [cuman].
tó-d·**æg**, *av*. to-day.
tó-dǽlan, *wv*. disperse ; separate, divide.
tó-g·**ædre**, *av*. together.
tó-g·**éanes**, *prp*. *w*. *dat*. towards—him tógéanes, to meet him.
tól, *sn*. tool.
tó-l·**íesan**, *wv*. loosen [léas].
tó-m·**iddes**, *prp*. *w*. *dat*. in the midst of.
tó-t·**eran**, *sv*. 4, tear to pieces.
tóþ, *sm*. tooth.
tó-weard, *aj*. future.
tó-w·**eorpan**, *sv*. 3, overthrow, destroy.
tréow, *sn*. tree.
get·**réowe**, *aj*. true, faithful.
trum, *aj*. strong.
trymman, *wv*. strengthen [trum].
trymmung, *sf*. strengthening, encouragement.
tucian, *wv*. ill-treat.
tugon, *see* **téon**.
tún, *sm*. village, town.
twá, **twám**, *see* **twegen**.
twegen, *num*. two.
twęlf, *num*. twelve.
twęntig, *num*. *w*. *gen*. twenty.

Þ.

þá, *av*. *cj*. then ; when—þá þá, when, while—*correlative* **þá** . . **þá**, when . . (then).
þá, **þám**, &c., *see* **se**.
þǽr, *av*. there—þǽrtó, &c. thereto, to it ; where—þǽr þǽr, *correl*. where.
þǽre, *see* **se**.
þǽr-rihte, *av*. immediately.
þæs, *av*. therefore ; wherefore.
þæs, **þæt**, *see* **se**.
þæt, *cj*. that.
geþ·**afian**, *wv*. allow, permit.
þá-g·**iet**, *av*. still, yet.
þanc, *sm*. thought ; thanks.
þancian, *wv*. *w*. *gen*. *of thing and dat*. *of person*, thank.

þanon, *av.* thence, away.
þás, *see* **þis**.
þe, *rel. prn.* who—se þe, who; *av.* when.
þé, *see* **þú**.
þéah, *av. cj.* though, yet, however —þéah þe, although.
þearf, *see* **þurfan**.
þearle, *av.* very, greatly.
þéaw, *sm.* custom, habit; þéawas, virtues, morality.
þegen, *sm.* thane; servant.
þegnian, *wv. w. dat.* serve.
þegnung, *sf.* service, retinue.
þęncan, *wv.* think, expect [þanc].
þéod, *sf.* people, nation.
*ge***þ·éode**, *sn.* language.
þéof, *sm.* thief.
þéos, *see* **þes**.
þéostru, *spl.* darkness.
þéow, *sm.* servant.
þéow-dóm, *sm.* service.
þéowian, *wv. w. dat.* serve.
þéowot, *sn.* servitude.
þes, *prn.* this.
þicce, *aj.* thick.
þicgan, *sv.* 5, take, receive; eat, drink.
þín, *see* **þú**.
þing, *sn.* thing.
þis, **þissum**, &c., *see* **þes**.
þóhte, *see* **þęncan**.
þone, *see* **se**.
þonne, *av. cj.* then; when; because.
þonne, *av.* than.
þorfte, *see* **þurfan**.
þorn, *sm.* thorn.
þrǽd, *sm.* thread.
þréo, *see* **þríe**.
þridda, *aj.* third.
þríe, *num.* three.
þrim, *see* **þríe**.
þritig, *num.* thirty.
þritig-feald, *aj.* thirtyfold.
þrymm, *sm.* glory.
þú, *prn.* thou.
þúhte, *see* **þyncan**.
*ge***þ·ungen**, *aj.* excellent, distinguished.
þurfan, *swv.* need.
þurh, *prp. w. acc.* through; *causal*, through, by.
þurh-w·unian, *wv.* continue.
þurst, *sm.* thirst.
þurstig, *aj.* thirsty.
þus, *av.* thus.
þúsend, *sn.* thousand.
*ge***þ·wǽr-lǽcan**, *wv.* agree.
þý, *instr. of* se; *av.* because.
þýfel, *sm.* bush.
þý·læs, *cj.* lest.
þyncan, *wv. impers. w. dat.* mé þyncþ, methinks [þęncan].
þyrel, *sn.* hole [þurh].

U.

Ufe-weard, *aj.* upward, at the top of.
un-árímed-lic, *aj.* innumerable.
unc, *see* **ic**.
un-gecynd, *aj.* strange, of alien family.
un-déad-lic-nes, *sf.* immortality.
under, *prp. w. dat. and acc.* under.
under-cyning, *sm.* under-king.
under-d·elfan, *sv.* dig under.
under-f·ón, *sv.* 1, receive, take.
under-g·ietan, *sv.* 5, understand.
undern-tíd, *sf.* morning-time.
un-forht, *aj.* dauntless.
un-for-molsnod, *aj.* (past partic.) undecayed.
un-gehíersum, *aj. w. dat.* disobedient.
un-gemetlic, *aj.* immense.
un-gerím, *sn.* countless number or quantity.
un-gerím, *aj.* countless.
un-gesǽlig, *aj.* unhappy, accursed.
un-hold, *aj.* hostile.
un-mihtig, *aj.* weak.
un-nytt, *aj.* useless.
un-rihtlice, *av.* wrongly.
un-rihtwís, *aj.* unrighteous.
un-scyldig, *aj.* innocent.
un-tíemend, *aj.* barren [*from pres. partic. of* tieman].
un-geþwǽr-nes, *sf.* discord.

un-*gewittig*, *aj.* foolish.
upp, *av.* up.
upp-áhafen-nes, *sf.* conceit, arrogance.
uppan, *prp. w. dat.* on, upon.
upp-flór, *sf.* (*dat. sing.* -a) upper floor, upper story.
urnon, *see* **iernan.**
ús, *see* **ic.**
út, *av.* out.
útan, *av.* outside.
uton. *defect. verb, w. infin.* let us—uton gán, let us go!

W.

Wacian, *wv.* be awake, watch.
wædla, *sm.* poor man.
wæl, *sn.* slaughter—wæl ges·léan, make a slaughter.
wæl-hréow, *aj.* cruel.
wælhréow-lice, *av.* cruelly.
wælhréownes, *sf.* cruelty.
wǽpen, *sn.* weapon.
wær, *aj.* wary.
wǽron, wæs, *see* **wesan.**
wæstm, *sm.* (growth); fruit.
wæter, *sn.* water.
wæter-scipe, *sm.* piece of water, water.
wáfung, *sf.* (spectacle), display.
-ware, *pl.* (only in composition) dwellers, inhabitants [*originally* defenders, *cp.* węrian].
wát, *see* **witan.**
gewát, *see* ***gewítan.***
wé, *see* **ic.**
***gew*·eald,** *sn.* power, command.
wealdan, *sv.* 1, *w. gen.* rule.
Wealh, *sm.* (*pl.* Wealas), *sm.* Welshman, Briton (*originally* foreigner).
weall, *sm.* wall.
weal-lím, *sm.* (wall-lime), cement, mortar.
wearg, *sm.* felon, criminal [*originally* wolf, *then* proscribed man, outlaw].
weaxan, *sv.* 1, grow, increase.
weg, *sm.* way, road.
weg-férende, *aj.* (pres. partic.) way-faring.
wel, *av.* well.
wel-willend-nes, *sf.* benevolence.
wénan, *wv.* expect, think.
***gew*·ęndan,** *wv.* turn; go [windan].
węnian, *wv.* accustom, wean [gewuna].
weofod, *sn.* altar.
weorc, *sn.* work.
weorpan, *sv.* 3, throw.
weorþ, *sn.* worth.
weorþ, *aj.* worth, worthy.
weorþan, *sv.* 3, happen; become—w. æt sprǽce, enter into conversation.
***gew*·eorþan,** *sv.* 3, *impers. w. dat.*—him gewearþ, they agreed on.
weorþ-full, *aj.* worthy.
weorþian, *wv.* honour, worship; make honoured, exalt.
weorþ-lice, *aj.* honourably.
weorþ-mynd, *sf.* honour.
wéox, *see* **weaxan.**
wépan, *sv.* 1, weep.
wer, *sm.* man.
węrian, *wv.* defend [wær].
werod, *sn.* troop, army.
wesan, *sv.* be.
west, *av.* west.
West-seaxe, *smpl.* West-saxons.
wéste, *aj.* waste, desolate.
wíd, *aj.* wide.
wíde, *av.* widely, far and wide.
widewe, *sf.* widow.
***gew*·ieldan,** *wv.* overpower, conquer [wealdan].
wierþe, *aj. w. gen.* worthy [weorþ].
wíf, *sn.* woman; wife.
wíf-healf, *sf.* female side.
wíf-mann, *sm.* woman.
wiht, *sf.* wight, creature, thing.
Wiht, *sf.* Isle of Wight [Vectis].
Wiht-ware, *pl.* Wight-dwellers [ware].
wilde, *aj.* wild.
wildéor, *sn.* wild beast.
willa, *sm.* will.
willan, *swv.* will, wish; *of repetition,* be used to.

*ge*w·**ilnian,** *wv. w. gen.* desire.
wín, *sn.* wine.
wind, *sm.* wind.
windan, *sv.* 3, wind.
wín-geard, *sm.* vineyard.
winnan, *sv.* 3, fight.
*ge*w·**innan,** *sv.* 3, win, gain.
winter (*pl.* winter), *sm.* winter; *in reckoning* = year.
winter-setl, *sn.* winter-quarters.
wís, *aj.* wise.
wíse, *sf.* (wise), way.
*ge*w·**iss,** *aj.* certain.
*ge*w·**issian,** *wv.* guide, direct.
*ge*w·**issung,** *sf.* guidance, direction.
wiste, *see* **witan.**
wit, *see* **ic.**
wita, *sm.* councillor, sage.
witan, *swv.* know.
*ge*w·**ítan,** *sv.* 6, depart.
wíte, *sn.* punishment; torment.
wítega, *sm.* prophet.
witod-líce, *av.* truly, indeed, and [witan].
*ge*w·**itt,** *sn.* wits, intelligence, understanding [witan].
wiþ, *prp. w. dat. and acc.* towards; along—wiþ weg, by the road; *hostility,* against—fuhton wiþ Brettas, fought with the Britons; *association, sharing,* &c., with; *defence,* against; *exchange, price, for*—wiþ þám þe, in consideration of, provided that.
wiþ-m·eten-nes, *sf.* comparison.
wiþ-s·acan, *sv.* 2, *w. dat.* deny.
wiþ-s·tandan, *sv.* 2, *w. dat.* withstand, resist.
wlite, *sm.* beauty.
wód, *aj.* mad.
wód-líce, *av.* madly.
wolde, *see* **willan.**
wóp, *sm.* weeping [wépan].
*ge***worden,** *see* **weorþan.**
word, *sn.* word; subject of talk, question, answer, report.
worhte, *see* **wyrcan.**
woruld, *sf.* world.
woruld-þing, *sn.* worldly thing.
wrecan, *sv.* 5, avenge.
wrégan, *wv.* accuse.
*ge*w·**rit,** *sn.* writing [wrítan].
wrítan, *sv.* 6, write.
wudu, *sm.* wood.
wuldor, *sn.* glory.
wuldrian, *wv.* glorify, extol.
wulf, *sm.* wolf.
*ge*w·**una,** *sm.* habit, custom [wunian].
wund, *sf.* wound.
wundor, *sn.* wonder; miracle.
wundor-líc, *aj.* wonderful, wondrous.
wundor-líce, *av.* wonderfully, wondrously.
wundrian, *wv. w. gen.* wonder.
*ge*w·**unelíc,** *aj.* customary.
wunian, *wv.* dwell, stay, continue [gewuna].
wunung, *sf.* dwelling.
*ge***wunnen,** *see ge***winnan.**
wyrcan, *wv.* work, make; build; do, perform [weorc].
wyrhta, *sm.* worker.
wyrt, *sf.* herb, spice; crop.
wyrt-brǽþ, *sm.* spice-fragrance, fragrant spice.
wyrtruma, *sm.* root.
wýscan, *wv.* wish.

Y.

Yfel, *aj.* evil, bad.
yfel, *sn.* evil.
ymbe, *prp. w. acc.* around; *of time,* about, at.
ymb-sc·rýdan, *wv.* clothe, array.
ymb-ú·tan, *av.* round about.
ýterra, *aj. comp.* outer; *superl.* ýtemest, outermost, last [út].

THE END.